D-DAY

Dedicated to my sons,
Ethan and Cameron.

D-DAY
JUNO BEACH

CANADA'S 24 HOURS OF DESTINY

LANCE GODDARD
FOREWORD BY MAJOR-GENERAL RICHARD ROHMER, D.F.C.

THE DUNDURN GROUP
TORONTO

Editor: Barry Jowett
Copy-Editor: Andrea Pruss
Design: Jennifer Scott
Printer: Friesens

National Library of Canada Cataloguing in Publication Data

Goddard, Lance
    D-Day : Juno Beach, Canada's 24 hours of destiny / Lance Goddard.

Includes bibliographical references.
ISBN 1-55002-492-2

1. World War, 1939-1945 — Campaigns — France — Normandy. 2. Canada. Canadian Army — History — World War, 1939-1945. I. Title.

D756.5.N6G62 2004   940.54'21422   C2004-900460-3

1   2   3   4   5   08   07   06   05   04

We acknowledge the support of the **Canada Council for the Arts** and the **Ontario Arts Council** for our publishing program. We also acknowledge the financial support of the **Government of Canada** through the **Book Publishing Industry Development Program** and **The Association for the Export of Canadian Books**, and the **Government of Ontario** through the **Ontario Book Publishers Tax Credit** program, and the **Ontario Media Development Corporation's Ontario Book Initiative.**

Care has been taken to trace the ownership of copyright material used in this book. The author and the publisher welcome any information enabling them to rectify any references or credit in subsequent editions.
                    J. Kirk Howard, President

Printed and bound in Canada.✪
Printed on recycled paper.

www.dundurn.com

Dundurn Press
8 Market Street
Suite 200
Toronto, Ontario, Canada
M5E 1M6

Gazelle Book Services Limited
White Cross Mills
Hightown, Lancaster, England
LA1 4X5

Dundurn Press
2250 Military Road
Tonawanda NY
U.S.A. 14150

"Confront them with annihilation and they will then survive. Plunge them into a deadly situation, and they will then live. When people fall into danger, they are then able to strive for victory."

~ Sun Tzu

TABLE OF CONTENTS

FOREWORD

The sixth day of June 1944 was D-Day. That day, starting just after 0001 hours, the first Canadian, British, and American paratroopers jumped out of their transport aircraft into the black darkness over Normandy. Their task was to open the long-expected attack against Hitler's Fortress Europa, an assault designed to liberate Western Europe from the oppressive, brutal, deadly, humanity-crushing rule of Nazi Germany.

The paratroopers of the 1st Canadian Parachute Battalion, a strong part of the combined Canadian-British force that jumped out of the Dakota and Albemarle aircraft, were the first Canadian troops to land on French soil on D-Day. Notwithstanding the horrendous handicap of the darkness and the confusion, the Canadians, while suffering major casualties, succeeded in gaining their assigned objectives east of the Orne River and north of Caen.

H-Hour was the time designated for the landing of Canadian, British, and American troops at their assigned beaches, starting from the Orne on the east and reaching miles to the west to Sword (British), Juno (Canadian), Gold (British), Omaha (American), and Utah (American).

At H-Hour, I was over the Canadian-British beaches at five hundred feet in my single-seater fighter reconnaissance RCAF Mustang 1 aircraft watching for attacking enemy Focke Wulfs and ME109s. At the same time I was taking in the incredible sight of the first landing craft approaching and hitting the beaches, and the distant-on-the-horizon smoke and winking flames of the battleships firing their huge shells at the enemy emplacements that I was flying over.

Now, sixty years later, comes this D-Day book, with its human, "I was there" descriptions of D-Day by surviving Canadian army, air force, and navy personnel on an hour-by-hour basis. It is an incredibly graphic tale from many Canadian mouths of what actually happened on that momentous day.

Lance Goddard's book will be published in advance of D-Day in its sixtieth anniversary year of 2004. This literary achievement, together with the many videotaped interviews by him of many of the now ancient young Canadian boys who took part in D-Day, is a rich accomplishment and a worthy recognition of the victories, the sacrifices, the achievements, the blood of injuries, and the deaths that came with the brave Canadians who arrived on D-Day in or over Normandy or on the waters of its approaches in the English Channel.

Richard Rohmer, Major-General, OC, CMM, DFC, QC
Flying Officer 430 Squadron, 39 Recce Wing, 2 Tactical Air Force, on D-Day: June 6, 1944.
Also Chair, the 60th Anniversary of D-Day Advisory Committee to the
Minister of Veterans Affairs.

430 Squadron (RR) Mustang P-51A over German vehicles at closing of Falaise Gap, August 19, 1944

THE MEN

Charles McNabb

Queen's Own Rifles C Company

Roy Shaw

Queen's Own Rifles B Company

Arthur Perry

7th Canadian Infantry Brigade

Mark Lockyer

1st Canadian Parachute Battalion B Company

Ed Reeve

Armoured Corp HQ

Charles Fosseneuve
13th Field Artillery Regiment 22nd Battery

Francis Godon
Royal Winnipeg Rifles B Company

August Herchenratter
Highland Light Infantry

Douglas Barrie
Highland Light Infantry

Roy Clarke
RCAF 419 Squadron

Hal Whitten
Royal Canadian Navy

Jim Parks
Royal Winnipeg Rifles

Rolph Jackson
Queen's Own Rifles B Company

Joe Oggy
Queen's Own Rifles B Company

John Turnbull
RCAF 419 & 424 Squadrons

Ernie Jeans
1st Canadian Parachute Battalion

Wilf Delaurie
1st Canadian Parachute Battalion

Richard Rohmer
RCAF Fighter Reconnaissance 430 Squadron

Jan de Vries
1st Canadian Parachute Battalion

Andrew Irwin
Royal Canadian Navy

William Kelly
RCAF 419 Squadron

Bob Dale
RCAF Squadron

Ken Hill
RCAF Squadron

Cecil Brown
RCAF 127 Spitfire Wing

Jack Martin
Queen's Own Rifles C Company

Wayne Arnold
1st Battalion Canadian Scottish Regiment

Jack Read
Royal Regina Rifles

Frank Ryan
North Shore (New Brunswick) Regiment

Don Learment
North Nova Scotia Highland Regiment

Arthur John Allin
Royal Canadian Artillery 14th Field Regiment

Philip John Cockburn
1st Hussars

Douglas Lavoie
Fort Garry Horse

John Dionne
17th Hussars

INTRODUCTION

This book is a companion piece to the documentary *D-Day: Canada's 24 Hours of Destiny*, which marks the sixtieth anniversary of D-Day with its broadcast on June 6, 2004, on Prime TV. While the documentary, like this book, covers D-Day on an hour-by-hour basis, time constraints will not allow me to air all of the interviews that I conducted for the production. Even the video release of the longer version of the documentary cannot reflect the scope of twenty hours of interviews on camera, and an additional ten hours of telephone interviews. Only a book allows all of the experiences of the veterans whom I talked with to be shared.

This project started late in 2002, when I completed work on *Victory From Above*, a documentary about the 1st Canadian Parachute Battalion. The show was well received, and sales for the video release were outstanding (part of the proceeds of the sales went to the Juno Beach Centre). Having completed such a satisfying project, I immediately pitched the idea of a D-Day documentary for the sixtieth anniversary, and it was quickly green-lighted. Production commenced in June 2003, shooting interviews in Normandy and covering the opening of the Juno Beach Centre.

What followed was a whirlwind of interviews back in Canada and the dual production of the documentary and this book. I have striven to make it a reflection of the Canadian experience of D-Day. I prefer to let the men tell the story, and what follows is a compilation of what they saw and did — the experiences of a number of men on that day. I tried to get as many representatives of the various Canadian units that participated in D-Day as possible, in order to give a sense of the broad scope of the invasion. There are so many stories that can be told, and these are but a few. It is in honour of these brave men, whose valour gained victory and freedom for the world, that I wanted to produce the documentary and write this book. I hope that it does justice to those young Canadians who sacrificed so much … those who came home to share these experiences with us and those who made the ultimate sacrifice and never made it back. Lest we forget.

Lance Goddard

PRELUDE TO D-DAY

In the course of human history there have been many pivotal events that shaped civilization. During the twentieth century, there were a number of these moments. The first flight, the invention of the atomic bomb, the moon landing — these all have significant historical importance. But only one event truly stands out for its impact on history. It has been recognized by historians as the single most important experience of the twentieth century. It is D-Day.

On June 6, 1944, the Allied forces of Britain, Canada, and the United States invaded Fortress Europa, thus signalling the beginning of the end of the Second World War. The importance of this event cannot be underestimated. It was not just the sheer size of the operation — it was the largest ever in history — but also what was being defeated.

The Nazis were the most heinous regime to ever take power on earth, a political party whose doctrine was based on racism. Their actions were evil, their intent vicious. To lose to Nazi Germany would have changed the face of civilization on earth. Countless millions, if not billions, of people would have been exterminated in the search for racial purity and superiority. Their quest for world domination was clear, and the prospect for the human race would have been very grim if the Nazis had indeed fulfilled their "manifest destiny." To stop them was to save the world.

Today it is hard to fathom what a young generation of men faced when going to war against such a foe. Motivation was abundant in the happy-go-lucky days of youth, but facing death was the catalyst that turned boys into men. Their lives were put on hold for five or six years. They had to face the horrors of war, where friends could perish in the blink of an eye. They were a generation of heroes.

The tribulations of the war reached back home, where shortages and rationing made everyone a part of the war effort. There was a drawing together of Canadian society in all facets of life; everyone worked together to defeat the common enemy. Industry grew as it fed the ever-hungry war machine. Emancipation in the workplace was accelerated due to a shortage of men in the workforce. The country grew up in many ways.

No other nation supported the war effort like Canada. With a population of only 11 million at the time, an incredible 1.1 million Canadians joined the armed forces. The support of industry was unparalleled. Canada became the safe haven for European royalty during the Nazi occupation of their countries. British Commonwealth Air Training flight schools were based in Canada and trained the aircrews that would fight in the RAF and RCAF. Canada was a major force in the Second World War, with a military that would be one of the strongest in the world by 1945. Indeed, by 1944, Canada was one of the three primary countries selected to participate in the invasion of Normandy on D-Day.

But how did the world reach such a desperate state, one that required a momentous event like D-Day?

Adolf Hitler exploited the economic, social, and political upheaval to gain power in Germany. His actions would lead to the deaths of 50 million people.

The series of events that led up to D-Day actually started with the end of the First World War. The Treaty of Versailles dictated that the Germans pay such ruinous reparations to the victors of the war that their economy was destroyed. A once-proud people was brought to its knees, without any glimmer of hope for a future.

Out of such despair arose a political party that promised a return to prosperity and pride. At first, many considered the National Socialists a joke, but their grassroots popularity grew, and on January 30, 1933, the Nazi party took power. Under great pressure, President Paul Hindenburg named Adolf Hitler the Chancellor of Germany. Thus began the reign of a totalitarian regime that would rule through propaganda and coercion. Within a month Hitler mentioned *lebensraum*, or living room, in a speech, which foreshadowed his plans to expand the German state. His promise of restoring Germany to its "rightful place" in Europe was an indicator of things to come.

On October 19, 1933, Germany withdrew from the League of Nations. Diplomacy was something that Hitler wanted to deal with on his own terms. By February, Germany was preparing for war. Industry flourished, and the country's economy boomed. Hitler was fulfilling his promise to restore Germany.

But not everything about the National Socialist party was rosy. Loyalty within the party was split. Ernst Rohm led the *Sturmabteilung* (SA), known as "the brownshirts." He was both popular and powerful, and was seen as a possible threat. Hitler wanted to consolidate his power, so in a well-orchestrated move, he had his *Schutzstaffel* (SS) forces execute a thousand opponents, many within the party — including Rohm. The date was June 30, 1934. It was the infamous Night of the Long Knives. Hitler had eliminated all political and military opposition in one fell swoop. The SS, led by Heinrich Himmler, had also become the most feared force within the country. With the death of President Hindenburg (at the age of eighty-seven) a month later, Hitler was able to

A demagogue with an incredible grasp of propaganda, Hitler captured the imagination of the German people. His flair for pomp and circumstance hid a darker initiative of racism and hatred.

The Nuremberg rally of 1935 flexed the kind of muscle that the Nazis had gained in two short years of being in power.

overthrow the constitutional government and grasp total power. Hitler was named *Führer*, and the salute of "Heil Hitler" resounded all over Germany.

In January 1935, Hitler's dream of restoring Germany began to come to fruition when the Saar region voted in favour of rejoining Germany in a plebiscite. In March it was restored to Germany. That same month the Nazis introduced compulsory military service. On March 16, the establishment of the Luftwaffe was announced, in clear violation of the Treaty of Versailles. But there were no diplomatic repercussions, as the world had other concerns (including being gripped in a worldwide depression). Within a year the German military had reoccupied the Rhineland. With overwhelming military superiority in the region, Germany began to flex its muscles. On March 12, 1938, Germany annexed Austria, creating the "Greater German Reich Groszdeutschland." Fearing that it would be next, Czechoslovakia mobilized its meagre army. Tensions in Europe were building.

To defuse the situation, British Prime Minister Neville Chamberlain visited Hitler in Berchtesgaden on September 15, 1938, and again on the thirtieth of that month at the Munich Conference. Appeasement came in the form of granting Germany the Sudetenland from Czechoslovakia, with Hitler promising future co-operation. "Peace in our time" was proclaimed.

Adolf Hitler was a charismatic speaker who could manipulate an audience with his powerful delivery and emotion. Here he speaks during the German election campaign of 1936.

Hitler's word to Chamberlain was soon broken. On March 15, 1939, German troops mobilized to occupy the Bohemia and Moravia regions of Czechoslovakia. A week later, Das Mermelgebiet was annexed by Germany. In April, alliances were being made when Britain and France guaranteed military help to Romania and Greece if they were attacked by Germany or Italy. Albania was invaded by Italy on April 7, and on May 22 Germany and Italy signed a formal alliance called the Pact of Steel.

As the summer of 1939 drew to a close, Germany had signed a non-aggression pact with Joseph Stalin and the Soviet Union. This pact guaranteed Hitler that he would have to fight a war on only one front, and it was a staggering blow to England and France. Late in August,

Hitler guaranteed the neutrality of Belgium, Holland, Denmark, Luxembourg, and Switzerland. Europe braced for war.

On September 1, 1939, Germany invaded Poland. It was the world's introduction to the *blitzkrieg.* Incredibly well coordinated tanks, aircraft, and motorized infantry attacked and overran the Poles with lightning fast speed. On September 3, war was declared by Britain, Canada, France, India, Australia, New Zealand, and South Africa. The Second World War had begun.

The United States remained neutral, officially making that its position in a statement on September 5. There was not the kind of public support that would have been needed to wage such a war, and President Roosevelt could not afford any unpopular, long-lasting actions with an election coming up in 1940. It would take a devastating blow for the American public to be aroused into a fighting state of mind.

On September 7, French troops took the offensive and crossed the German border along the Saar front. On September 17, the Russians invaded Poland from the east, and by September 27, Warsaw had surrendered. At that point the Russians and Germans signed a friendship treaty that split Poland up between them. As Hitler had planned, the Germans had to concern themselves with only a one-front war in the west.

As 1940 began, so did rationing in England and France. They were brutally unprepared for the war. The superiority of the battle-tested German equipment showed up everywhere — in the air, on the land, and in the sea. In the spring the Germans shocked the Allies by invading Denmark and Norway. It was a disastrous campaign from the Allied perspective, and Prime Minister Neville Chamberlain was paying the price in Parliament. On May 10 he resigned, his career destroyed. Enter Britain's new prime minister, a man whose military background would serve him well in the years ahead, and whose personality was marked by a tenacity that would have him characterized as a "bulldog." Winston Churchill would be exactly the type of leader that Britain needed.

May 10 was a day that few would forget. Not because of the shift of power in the British Parliament, but because of what was happening in Europe. Operation Gelb saw the invasion of the neutral countries of Europe by the Nazis. The German blitzkrieg rolled through Holland, Luxembourg, and Belgium. Resistance lasted mere days (in Belgium's case weeks). Two days prior to the Belgian surrender, the trapped British troops were rescued at Dunkirk in Operation Dynamo. Nearly 338,000 troops were evacuated to England by a flotilla made up of naval and civilian craft. Not only was the withdrawal from the continent a devastating blow to their morale, but it also raised the spectre of an even greater impending danger: the invasion of England.

On June 14, the Germans marched into Paris. The following day the French abandoned the Maginot Line, and a week later France fell to Germany. The German navy had taken control of the shipping lanes of Northern Europe — and Britain was totally isolated. To force England to its knees, the Germans began a massive air assault against Britain — the Battle of Britain. The Luftwaffe had vastly superior numbers, and the Blitz bombing wreaked havoc and exacted a massive death toll amongst the civilians. But the British would not break. The success of the Royal Air Force in the Battle of Britain (with many Canadians in Spitfires and Hurricanes) led Hitler to postpone Operation Sea Lion on October 12. The invasion of England was not to be.

As 1941 was ushered in, Britain faced an even greater disaster. By January 10, the country was nearly bankrupt. But as bleak as the moment was, Britain had a friend: President Roosevelt had the Lend-Lease bill presented to the U.S. Congress. It would allow the United States to supply the British with much-needed military hardware and material without receiving payment for it immediately — if at all. It was the lifeline that Britain so desperately needed.

By April 1941, Germany and Italy controlled almost all of Europe. Britain held out in the west, while Russia was quietly bordering the east. May saw the British suffering heavy losses in North Africa as Rommel pushed them across the desert, and Operation Merkur left Crete surrendered to the Nazis. There was little going right for the Allies at the time.

But all this success did not sit well with Hitler. He felt that he had the British on their knees, and that he could divert his attention elsewhere. On June 22, 1941, Hitler began one of his biggest mistakes. With Operation Barbarossa, the Germans declared war on Russia and invaded all along the frontier — thus opening up a second front. Hitler had been critical of the Kaiser for his decision to fight a two-front war during the First World War. Now he was going to make the same mistake. The problem with fighting Russia was that the Eastern Front would be two thousand miles long. Despite the fact that Italy, Finland, and Romania joined the Germans in this campaign, it was doomed to failure ... eventually. What Russia lacked in materials, it more than made up for in manpower. Stalin would be able to throw millions of troops at the Germans. Then there was the vastness of Russia, creating long distances for the Germans to supply their armies at the front. It was a campaign that would have to march all the way to Asia to be successful, and the Germans simply didn't have enough soldiers and equipment to do that. Hitler would pay the price, but it would take time before the bill would come due.

While the war was being played out in Europe and North Africa, in Asia the Japanese were about to make it a truly global affair. On December 7, 1941, the Japanese attacked Pearl Harbor, devastating the U.S. Pacific Fleet and killing 2,344 people. It was the event that would galvanize the American nation and draw it into the war. On December 8, the United States declared war on Japan, as did Britain. On December 11, Germany and Italy signed an alliance with Japan and immediately declared war on the U.S.

The Germans were very aware of the precarious situation of their oil supply. Yet the rich oil fields of Russia would answer their needs, and make them a virtually unstoppable force. The vast Soviet supply of petroleum was beckoning from just beyond Stalingrad. The Russians knew that would be the pivotal site. So did the Germans. It also became a battle of wills between Hitler and Stalin — ideology versus ideology, with the prize being the city named after Stalin himself. On September 15, 1942, the Battle of Stalingrad began. It was one of the bloodiest, most vicious engagements in the war. The stakes were high, and both sides were willing to pay that high price in blood.

The low point in Canada's involvement in the Second World War: Dieppe. Landing craft move in during Operation Jubilee, delivering the men to shore — and to their unfortunate fate.

The toll for Dieppe was steep, paid for with Canadian blood.

German officers survey the damage among the dead and wounded of Canada's army.

As the Germans pressed deeper into Russia, they also had to contend with holding the continent along the western coast of Europe. For an invasion to succeed, the force would have to land where it had access to a port. This would enable the invaders to immediately supply their forces and not be driven back into the ocean. The only problem was that the Nazis knew this as well, and they heavily fortified every port along the Atlantic Coast. But an experimental landing had to be attempted, and the mission was given to the Canadians and British. The target: Dieppe. The date: August 19, 1942. What happened can be attributed to many causes: the lack of air support, the poorly planned location (since the pebble beach gave the armoured vehicles no traction), the massive artillery advantage held by the Germans, and the lack of surprise. The final result was catastrophic. An abject failure coupled with massive losses to the Canadian and British military signalled one of the lowest points in the war.

Without the ability to invade Europe, the Allies could not go on the offensive. Without going on the offensive, an army cannot win a war. So the mistakes made at Dieppe had to be studied to avoid another disaster in the future. The lesson of Dieppe was that a German-held port could not be taken head-on, so a mobile port would have to be built and towed across to France with the invading Allied force. On May 12, 1943, the Trident Conference was held by the Allies to discuss an invasion across the English Channel. British General Sir Frederick Morgan was named the chief planner of the operation, and his target date was May 1, 1944. He had just under a year to plan a massive operation that would coordinate all of the branches of the military service in order to land somewhere along the Atlantic Coast. It was to be called Operation Overlord. And so the planning began …

Successful amphibious landings were nearly unprecedented in military history, yet prior to D-Day the Allies had managed to succeed at three attempts. One of these occurred on July 9 and 10, 1943. Operation Husky saw a massive airborne/amphibious attack on Sicily, where

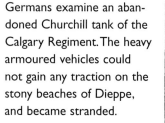

Germans examine an abandoned Churchill tank of the Calgary Regiment. The heavy armoured vehicles could not gain any traction on the stony beaches of Dieppe, and became stranded.

3,000 ships and landing craft delivered 8 divisions of troops (160,000 men), along with 14,000 vehicles, 600 tanks, and 1,800 artillery guns. It was a well-executed invasion that overwhelmed the defenders of Sicily, and the entire island was in Allied hands by August 17.

On August 13, President Roosevelt and Prime Minister Churchill met in

Quebec to discuss the preliminary plans for the invasion of Europe. With the invasion of Sicily well underway, their focus was to get their troops into northwestern Europe and end the war. It was during this conference that it was decided that Operation Overlord would be led by an American. Who it would be was Roosevelt's decision.

On November 28, 1943, Roosevelt, Churchill, and Stalin met at the Teheran Conference to coordinate their military efforts. Some of the discussions were about Operation Overlord, with Stalin committing to an offence at the same time to prevent the Germans from transferring forces from the Eastern to the Western Front.

On Christmas Eve, 1943, General Eisenhower was named the Supreme Commander of the Allied Expeditionary Forces. His ability to work with both the British and American military commanders made him an excellent choice. His leadership abilities were impeccable.

The superiority of the air war was shifting as well. The USAAF began to fill the daytime skies with aircraft, while the RAF and RCAF bombers worked effectually at night. The Germans could not produce aircraft at the speed that the Allies did. The Americans and Canadians built their

Canadian prisoners were shackled and marched through the streets of Dieppe by the Germans. The treatment of these men enraged the Canadian forces and motivated them to find an opportunity to pay the Germans back. They would have to wait almost two years.

Many of the men who participated in D-Day had friends or family members involved in the Dieppe raid. For them, it was personal.

Some of the lucky few who made it back home, injured and dejected.

With Operation Jubilee a shattering failure, the downtrodden soldiers return to England, filled with worry about what the future of the war would hold.

aircraft in the safety of North American factories, while the British continued to build their own bombers, Spitfires, and other combat aircraft. On the other hand, the German factories were bombed with regularity. The Allies secured fuel supplies and could transport them by sea with less danger now that the U-Boat offensive was diminishing. The Germans' source of fuel was being choked off by the continual bombing of the Ploesti oil fields of Romania. The results were showing up on the battlefield.

The Germans were being squeezed, but one final blow was needed to mortally wound them: an attack from the west, one that could rapidly strike at the industrial heartland of Germany. A bold move that would create another front — one that would make it impossible for the Germans to defend everything. The Nazis still controlled a huge portion of Europe, and it would take a major campaign to bring the war to an end. It was time for the decisive blow known as Operation Overlord.

PREPARATION FOR D-DAY

The Atlantic Wall

In March 1942, Hitler laid out the parameters of Directive 40 for the development of the Atlantic Coast defences. The plan was to create an Atlantic Wall — a series of interlocking defences made up of bombproof concrete bunkers and trenches that would cover the entire coastline. Hitler envisioned fifteen thousand concrete strongpoints manned by three hundred thousand troops. The wall would stretch thousands of kilometres from Spain to Norway, protected by mines, barbed wire, flamethrowers, and tank ditches. The bunkers were gas proof, with double doors and a filtration system. If all else failed, there were armoured doors and escape tunnels. Smaller Tobruk gun emplacements gave the German troops a concrete gun position complete with underground supplies. The guns were positioned to fire across the beaches from two sides, creating a crossfire that was impossible to avoid. No stretch of beach would go undefended. All positions were targeted. It would be a formidable obstacle — the largest built since the Great Wall of China.

The concept of the Atlantic Wall was simple: no site would be safe to land an invasion force. The defences along the shoreline would repel a landing. Larger gun emplacements would target the supply ships offshore. Hitler wanted it completed by May 1, 1943, but that was not to be. Given the lack of supplies and manpower — plus the magnitude of the project — it could not possibly be completed by that date. Local contractors were hired to build the defences, and slave labour was also used; in total, 260,000 men worked on the project. Over 17 million cubic tonnes of concrete were used to create the emplacements. With such a huge amount of coastline to defend, and work not progressing as anticipated, the Germans decided to focus on protecting the most likely landing sites.

Calais was the obvious target. It was the shortest distance for the Allies to cross the Channel, and there was a port — something vital for an amphibious landing to deliver supplies. To ensure that the Allies would target Calais, Hitler made the area the launching site for his V-1 flying bombs (which began to hit London on June 12, 1944) and later for his V-2 rockets. The Germans fortified Calais with the formidable 88mm anti-aircraft and anti-tank guns to ensure that it was impregnable. The trap was set.

However, the Germans were not unanimous about the planned defences. Concerned about the damage a naval bombardment could do, the German commander in Western Europe, Field Marshal von Rundstedt, was uncomfortable with putting everything into the coastal defences. His desire was to hold back the armoured divisions inland and to use them as a force for a mobile counterattack. But Field Marshal Erwin Rommel was put in charge of the Atlantic Wall defences under von Rundstedt in November 1943. He favoured putting everything up on the coast to prevent the Allies from setting foot on the shore. Hitler decided on a compromise between the two and split the command in the region between Rommel and von Rundstedt. Hitler himself would control the Panzers. Hitler's division of military power was a surprising decision for someone who centralized political power, and it would prove disastrous. On the morning of D-Day, a counterattack could not be launched by the Panzers since Hitler had slept in (and no one dared to wake him).

Rommel had the beaches of Normandy littered with mines and obstacles in a vain attempt to turn back an Allied invasion.

Rommel set about increasing the fortifications along the coast. He had more and more concrete poured. He visited the sites and adjusted the plans. He had more mines laid offshore. Belgian gates — tidal flat obstacles running parallel to the coastline with mines attached — were installed about 150 metres from the high water point. About one hundred metres out, logs were embedded in the sand at an angle facing out to sea, also with mines attached. In addition, hedgehogs — metal crosses designed to rip out the bottoms of landing craft — were positioned along the coast about seventy metres out. These mines and obstacles were intended to destroy landing craft as they moved towards the shore. Rommel believed that a landing would happen at high tide, and this belief determined the placement of the mines. It was a miscalculation: while the obstacles were dangerous to the Allies on D-Day, the landings took place at low tide, and so many of the carefully placed deterrents were exposed and out of the water during the landings.

The German Army

By 1944, Germany controlled more territory than it could defend. Hitler did not want to give up an inch of land, so his resources were stretched incredibly thin. The Eastern Front stretched from the Baltic to the Black Sea, the south was a combination of a front in Italy and a long Mediterranean coastline, and the Western Front was a coastline that stretched from Spain to Norway. The Germans faced shortages of every kind — not only men, but also ships, aircraft, guns, and tanks. They had changed their approach to the war due to these shortages, from the highly mobile blitzkrieg to a slow and dug-in occupational force.

The Germans were facing massive casualties on the Eastern Front. It had become clear by early 1944 that it was a war they could not win. Hitler knew that his only hope was to get the Russians to break their treaty with the Allies and withdraw from the war. To push Stalin to such a decision would require the ability to inflict heavy damage on the Russians — something that would be difficult with the resources available to Hitler on the Eastern Front. He would need to take troops from the western coastal defence to do so. But that made him vulnerable to attack from the British, Canadians, and Americans stationed in Britain, as well as their Polish, Norwegian, and other allies.

So Hitler's focus turned west in early 1944. An invasion along the western European coast would be far more dangerous to the Germans than an advance from the east. The western coast was within striking distance of the Rhine-Ruhr industrial heartland of Germany. An advance of the same distance by the Russians would find them still out of reach of Berlin or any other vital centre. The key to the war was defending the coastline, and Hitler realized that to defeat a landing would not only seriously demoralize the Allies, it would set them back months, if not years, and would reduce the threat of another invasion for a long time. That time then could be spent eliminating the Russians from the war.

Hitler recognized the importance of the invasion so much that he was quoted as saying, "The destruction of the enemy's landing attempt means more than a purely local decision on the Western Front. It is the sole decisive factor in the whole conduct of the war and hence its final result."

For such a pivotal site, the defences were lacking. It was a reflection of the shortages that the Germans faced. The English Channel and other waters of the Western Front were patrolled solely by E-Boats, fast patrol craft that could do damage but would not last long in any extended engagements. Unfortunately there were few E-Boats available, and much of the coastal defence was left to mines. The Germans could not depend on the Luftwaffe to aid in the defence of the coast; by 1944 they were vastly outnumbered in the skies by the Allies, and their shortage of fuel was dealing the German air force a devastating blow. Without a strong navy or air force, the Germans were essentially blind. They would not be able to see a buildup of force, and they would have no idea where the invasion force was heading. The bottom line was that the Germans could only guess where the landing would take place, and even then they would only know for sure once the invasion force was spotted from the shoreline. At that point it would be too late to move in reinforcements. The Germans would have to prepare for a landing anywhere along the twenty-six-hundred-kilometre-long coast.

The biggest concern for the Germans was a shortage of men, and while the buildup of fixed fortifications was intended to repel a landing right on the beach, the staggering losses on the Eastern Front — 3 million casualties — meant they'd have to look elsewhere for soldiers to man the emplacements. They could no longer continue to fight only with the "racially pure." Soldiers were conscripted from the occupied territories and from the ranks of the POWs. Some were willing to fight against the Communists. Others were drawn by the better rations given to soldiers over POWs. Some had been conscripted by the Russians elsewhere and had no real allegiances in the first place. But these *Ost* (East) troops were not as well trained, nor as motivated, as the German troops. After the battle of Kursk, it became obvious that they could not be depended on along the Eastern Front, so they were exchanged with German troops in France. By D-Day, one in six defenders along the coast were Ost troops. This lack of quality troops led the German officers in charge to command with a pistol in hand. Motivation was a bullet.

The Ost units were used to man the fixed fortifications. The counterattacks would be handled by the Waffen-SS. There were no issues with the quality of the Waffen-SS. They were crack troops, loyal until death (many had grown up in the Hitler Youth), utterly vicious, and with no concept of surrender. But there were few units available of the Waffen-SS, and they were spread out strategically, prepared to strike where needed.

The Allies

For the Allies, the invasion was a necessity. An army cannot win a war without going on the offensive. Also, Stalin wanted another front to take the pressure off of his troops. For years the Russians had faced the Germans on the ground alone in Europe, and they were growing weary of the huge losses.

The Allies needed surprise, and they needed to land where they could reinforce, supply, and expand immediately. They had learned from the Dieppe disaster not to attempt a landing at a well-fortified port, which immediately eliminated Calais from consideration. Amphibious landings were difficult at best, with few historical successes. The Allies had amazingly already accomplished three landings in the war (North Africa in 1942, Sicily in July 1943, and Salerno in September 1943), but this time it was different. They were expected, and the Germans were well fortified with the Atlantic Wall.

The choice of landing sites was determined by several factors. The site had to be within a reasonable distance of England for shipping

Left: Stranded tanks at Dieppe. The Allies learned a number of valuable lessons from the failure of that raid.

Below: Amphibious assaults on a fortified port proved disastrous at Dieppe, and many Canadian men paid with either their freedom or their lives.

supplies and for air support. It had to be within striking distance of the Rhine-Ruhr region (the ultimate objective of the campaign). It had to be in a concentrated area, since there could only be six divisions landed (due to the limited number of landing craft available). The landing area had to be able to allow armoured vehicles to gain traction and move forward (unlike Dieppe). The area had to be able to support the immediate delivery of supplies and reinforcements (like a port). These prerequisites narrowed down the possibilities considerably.

Calais had already been ruled out as being too well defended. Le Havre was too difficult and would have meant splitting the invasion force between the two sides of the river, reducing their effectiveness and increasing the opportunity to be defeated. Brittany was too far and out of the range of the air force fighters. Holland and Belgium were ruled out since they could easily be flooded and defended. They were also too close to Luftwaffe airbases. Through the process of elimination, Normandy was chosen as the site for the landings.

The Calvados coast was ideal. It had long beaches to land on, small ports to bring in supplies (as well, two huge prefabricated ports could be built there), and sites where many tactical airfields could be quickly developed to start delivering supplies and launching aerial attacks once the area was captured. The site was within striking distance of Paris, and it had the added advantage of the Orne River — a geographical boundary that divided the German army, thus weakening it. The Allies also had excellent reconnaissance of the region. They controlled the skies, so they had a multitude of photos of the area and its emplacements. In addition, the French Resistance had supplied extensive, detailed information about the Atlantic Wall, the defenders, the lines of communication, and much more. The Allies knew exactly what they were up against.

In fear of repeating the debacle at Dieppe, it was decided to find out whether the beaches along the Normandy shore could support the weight of the vehicles that were to land there and give them traction to move inland. A series of missions to the beaches was carried out. A midget submarine was sent into shore all along the proposed landing sites to take soil samples. Under cover of darkness the men swam ashore and drove long tubes into the beaches to look at the different layers of material that made up each of the sites. These samples were examined back in England to determine whether the beaches could support the landings and the weight of the vehicles. Several missions were carried out, commencing on December 31, 1943. The results were promising, but the reports also pointed out how well fortified the beaches were.

The Plan

The plan for Operation Overlord was broken down over five beaches. From west to east, the landings were planned as such: the Americans would land at Utah and Omaha beaches, then the British at Gold Beach, the Canadians at Juno Beach, and the British at Sword Beach, towards the Orne. The landings would be over seventy miles of shoreline. The U.S. Airborne would parachute in and cover the right flank (looking south). Similarly, the British 6th Airborne (including the 1st Canadian Parachute Battalion) would drop to the east of the Orne and Dives rivers and cover the left flank. The first wave to hit the beach was intended to disable the German defences along the Atlantic Wall, and the follow-up waves would pour inland to capture strategic positions. The RAF and RCAF bombers were to fly in overnight and hit the fortifications along the beaches and inland to soften the targets. The navy was to hit the shoreline targets with an artillery barrage early in the morning — prior to and during the actual landings. It was expected that little would be left of the German fortifications. The navy would then provide artillery support for the remainder of the day. The plan was huge, dependent on precise timing, and highly ambitious in its goals.

For the Canadians, the D-Day assignment went to the 3rd Division, under the command of Major General Rod Keller. The plan was broken down over two sectors: Mike (comprising Red and Green sections) to the west and Nan (Red, Green, and White sections) to the east. Fictitious names were used so that the troops did not know where they would be landing. Mike sector was to the west and included the town of Courseulles-sur-Mer. This would be the target of the 7th Canadian Brigade Group under Brigadier Harry Foster. The Royal Winnipeg Rifles were to land west of the Seulles River on beaches protected by several concrete emplacements. The Canadian Scottish were to land west of the Royal Winnipeg Rifles. The Royal Regina Rifles (with support from the tanks of the 1st Hussars) were to land on the beaches in front of Courseulles and clear the town of Germans. Nan Sector was the eastern section of Juno Beach and included the towns of Bernières-sur-Mer and St. Aubin-sur-Mer; it was split into two major landing

The Allied commanders of Operation Overlord, a combination of American and British senior officers. In the front row (l-r): Air Chief Marshal Sir Arthur Tedder, General Dwight Eisenhower (Supreme Commander), General Sir Bernard Montgomery. In the back row (l-r): General Omar Bradley, Admiral Sir B. Ramsay, and Air Chief Marshal Sir Trafford Leigh-Mallory.

sites. Brigadier K.G. Blackader would command the 8th Canadian Brigade Group there. The Queen's Own Rifles were to land at Bernières-sur-Mer and take the small beachfront town. It was well defended with pillboxes and a seawall that cut off exits from the beach. St. Aubin-sur-Mer was the mission of the North Shore (New Brunswick) Regiment. The Fort Garry Horse Armour was to support both landings. In reserve was Le Régiment de la Chaudière from Quebec. Once the beaches had been cleared, a second wave would land and begin the movement inland. Amongst the second wave were the Stormont, Dundas, and Glengarry Highlanders, the North Nova Scotia Highlanders, the Highland Light Infantry, and the Sherbrooke Fusiliers. In addition to the infantry units, there were also a multitude of support units landing. While Juno Beach was not heavily covered with concrete emplacements, it was well defended. The beaches were littered with obstacles, and seawalls created natural defences that favoured the Germans. There were no natural obstacles along Juno Beach, just sand dunes. The landing would be delayed by a half-hour (in comparison with the other beaches) to allow the tide to come in enough to clear the offshore reef. But there was no perfect time to land at Juno — arriving later, while clearing the reef, meant landing amongst the obstacles, most of which had mines attached to them. However, a later landing would also reduce the vast amount of beach that the men would have to race across under heavy fire. These were fishing towns with vacation homes along the shore — buildings that gave the Germans a large number of vantage points along the shoreline.

The other Canadians participating in D-Day had various roles to play. The 1st Canadian Parachute Battalion was attached to the British 6th Airborne and had several objectives to meet in the early hours of D-Day morning. They were to eliminate the guns at the Merville battery (which could reach Ouistreham and the British on Sword Beach), remove a German command post at Varaville and a battery nearby, blow up bridges along the Dives River, and then protect

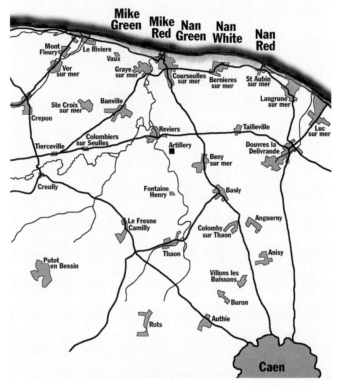

Group photo of the senior officers of the 3rd Canadian Infantry Division who participated in D-Day. Major General R.F. Keller was highly popular with the Canadian men, and is situated fourth from the left in the front row.

the left flank of the invasion by positioning themselves in force at Le Mesnil. The Canadians in the RCAF flew more than a thousand bomber sorties that targeted the batteries at Merville, Franceville, and Houlgate. Some were given the task of bombing the German emplacements along the Atlantic Wall to soften them up for the landings. Canadian pilots in the 2nd Tactical Air Force would fly during the invasion and throughout the day to provide protection from the Luftwaffe, visual and photo reconnaissance, and some fire support. The Royal Canadian Navy participated in Operation

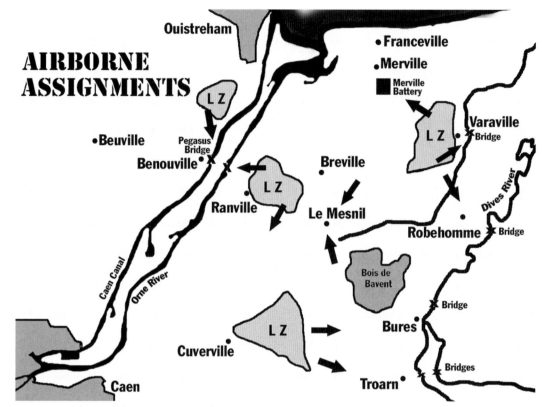

Neptune (the naval component of Operation Overlord) by minesweeping early on for the British, Canadian, and American beaches to secure safe lanes to the invasion sites for the landing craft carrying troops to Normandy. RCN ships also took part in the artillery barrage that immediately preceded the landings on the beaches as well as in the ongoing artillery support during the advance inland.

The Canadian participation in D-Day was vital. One of only three major national invading forces, the Canadians were given the objectives of moving across Highway 13 to the Paris-Cherbourg railway line as well as seizing Carpiquet airport — an airfield that would be important to the ongoing success of the invasion. It was a difficult task. Canada was to be a major player in this pivotal moment of the twentieth century.

Due to the importance of the operation, it was planned and trained for under the utmost secrecy. To deceive the Germans, a bogus plan was devised: Operation Fortitude, under General George S. Patton, whom the Germans regarded as the best Allied general. It too was huge in scope and planning. It made it appear to the Germans that the big invasion was being planned for the Pas de Calais area or even Norway. Fictitious divisions and landing craft were created, and information was leaked via radio and double agents. There were enough intercepted communications about Fortitude that the Germans took it to be real. Several divisions were moved to Norway in anticipation of an invasion, rather than being stationed in France.

But things changed on April 27, 1944. Operation Tiger had the Allied troops performing landing exercises at Slapton Sands when they were attacked by German E-Boats. Two landing ship tanks (LSTs) were sunk. The loss of seven hundred American lives was tragic. Even worse was the fact that the incident brought something to Hitler's attention: the beaches at Slapton Sands were extraordinarily similar to those in Normandy. Hitler immediately ordered the reinforcement of the defences in Normandy. For the Allies, the time to invade was sooner rather than later. With the Germans fortifying their positions, the longer the Allies waited to invade, the worse it was going to be to overcome the Atlantic Wall.

Despite the pressure to invade on the originally planned date of May 1, General Eisenhower decided to postpone the operation one month in order to get extra production of landing craft. A number of different landing craft had been designed for just such an operation. As well as the LST, other landing craft, including the LCT (landing craft tank), the LCI (landing craft infantry), the LCA (landing craft assault), and the LCVP (landing craft vehicles and personnel), were all going to play a prominent role on D-Day. They all had a shallow draught and were ideal for the conditions along the Normandy coast. As necessity is the mother of invention, several other interesting designs were used. Duplex Drive tanks, known as DD tanks, had inflatable tubes and canvas sides that allowed them to float and power ashore on their own (to arrive onshore in advance of the infantry troops in order to eliminate the pillboxes and emplacements). Hobart's Funnies were various devices added to tanks to overcome ditches and obstacles and to clear paths from mines, to name but a few uses. These designs were from the British army and were primarily used by British and Canadian troops, saving many lives in the process.

The timing of the invasion was a source of debate amongst the commanders of the different branches of the military. The navy wanted a daylight landing to avoid confusion and collisions among the multitude of ships and landing craft that were going to be involved in the operation. The air force also wanted a daylight landing to guarantee the accuracy of their bomb runs and fire support. The army, on the other hand, wanted to land at first light. It would afford the soldiers surprise up to the moment of landing, and it would give them an entire day to achieve their objectives and solidify their positions. In the end, the army's concerns were recognized, and the plan was to land at first light.

Another major consideration for the Allies was the combination of tidal and lunar conditions. It was necessary to land on a rising tide. It would allow the landing craft to run ashore, unload, and then float away with the tide. The landing craft could then ferry fresh troops in and the wounded out on each trip to shore. In recognition of the navy's concerns about accidents on the crossing with so many ships involved, it was determined that the crossing would occur during a minimum of a half-moon for illumination. The combination of the two conditions narrowed down the possible dates of the invasion to June 5, 6, and 7 or June 19 and 20. The decision was made to go on June 5, 1944.

The Allies wanted to have the element of surprise on their side for the invasion. One miscalculation by Rommel gave it to them: he felt sure that the invasion would be on a high tide. By his calculations, the soonest date possible for all of the conditions to be perfect was June 20. The Germans were not at a heightened level of preparedness early in June. In fact, as the date of invasion arrived, Rommel was in Germany celebrating his wife's birthday, the majority of the commanders were at a war games meeting, and the troops were comfortably enjoying a peaceful occupation. Surprise indeed played a part, and it was completely in favour of the Allies.

The one thing that was beyond the control of the Allies was the weather. It turned bad as D-Day approached, and the invasion on June 5 was postponed. The men were on their ships and landing craft, ready and anxious to go. Years of waiting and training had them prepared, and now all they wanted was to see some action. It was time to take an active role in the war.

Then late on the fifth the meteorological unit came up with what Eisenhower was waiting for: a break in the weather. It would get better in time for the landings the next morning. And so Eisenhower, with his American and British commanders, decided: June 6, 1944, would be D-Day. It was the greatest seaborne operation in military history. There had never been a larger armada of naval craft. Nothing of the magnitude of this endeavour had ever been attempted before. It involved the joint efforts of the Allied armies, navies, and air forces in a precisely coordinated action that would turn the tide of the war and change history forever.

On the night of June 5, the ships were loaded with men and equipment, the bombers flew their sorties, and the airborne boarded their aircraft to embark on the great crusade. The two prefabricated Mulberry ports were ready to be towed across to Normandy and sunk at predetermined sites at the British and American beaches. One hundred thirty thousand men were to land over the next twenty-four hours, to invade Europe and rid it of the Nazi menace. The most important event of the twentieth century was about to begin.

READY TO GO

Don Learment, North Nova Scotia Highland Regiment

There was a tremendous relief on the part of everybody — "We've waited this long, now it's here, let's see what we can do." After all that time. And we were pretty finely trained — but we were green troops going into action in a strange country. Almost no one had been under enemy fire at all.

Doug Barrie, Highland Light Infantry

We were all excited of course. We knew it was coming and we were anxious to take part in it. We knew it was going to be an historic day and we had been chomping at the bit for a long time in Britain — some had been over there for four years getting prepared for this. We were in good shape and our morale was very high. The only thing, of course, is that you have a little trepidation and you just wonder how it's going to turn out. You're anxious to get going but you're not sure what's going to happen, and where you're going to be, and whether you'll

Top Left: The men of the Highland Light Infantry load up onto an LCI (L) in preparation for the crossing of the English Channel.

Top Right: The men of the 1st Canadian Parachute Battalion (attached to the British 6th Airborne) in full battle dress and waiting to load onto the airplanes.

Centre Left: Ready to embark, a large fleet of LCTs loaded with supplies for the invasion made up just a small part of a massive armada that would descend upon the Normandy coast.

Centre Right: A large number of the Canadian troops crossed the English Channel on larger ships, such as the HMCS *Prince David*. The men of Le Régiment de la Chaudière climb up the scramble ropes to board the ship for their crossing.

Bottom Left: Loaded aboard LCI (L) 262, Canadian soldiers wait for Operation Overlord to get underway. Sergeant Pete Huffman inspects the rifle of Private John Thomas.

come through okay. It was a little easier for an officer because you had the men under you to consider and to look after, and so that sort of took your mind off a lot of the worry.

ONTARIO PARATROOPERS IN THEIR FINAL, TENSE MOMENTS AS THEY AWAITED INVASION'S TAKE-OFF ORDER

COMPANY COMMANDER Major Fuller of Toronto gives final orders to C.S.M. W. I. Blair of Peterboro as Canadian paratroopers prepared to take off for France on D-Day.

FORMER LIGHT opera singer, Sergt. George Capraru of Toronto, paratroop sniper, makes final adjustments to his kit before take-off time.

R.S.M. W. J. CLARK of Ottawa checks over last-minute instructions with C.S.M. N. Joseph of Cornwall. These Canadian paratroopers landed and fought near Caen.

PTE. J. T. CHURCH   PTE. P. BISMUTKA   PTE. W. CHADDOCK

PTE. A. HOGARTH   PTE. W. MIDDLETON   PTE. W. MURRAY

AMONG THE FIRST to land were these Toronto sky soldiers. Privates Bismutka and Hogarth are tankmen; Middleton is a sniper. Church a bomber.

Jim Parks, Royal Winnipeg Rifles

Oh yeah, we had been preparing for what they called a "second front" for quite a few years, and to us that's what it was: a second front. Even in 1942 in the Dieppe raid we thought it was going to be the second front. We knew from what we were told by the current affairs officers (and what we would read in the newspaper) how important it was to launch a second front as soon as possible. Later on we found out they tried to have it in 1943 but it was put off until 1944. We'd been comman-

Top: Newspapers covered D-Day from every angle, including the preparations by Canada's first battalion of paratroopers.

Centre: A group of Canadian paratroopers having a warm drink before loading onto their aircraft.

Bottom: Two members of the 14th Field Regiment of the Royal Canadian Artillery inspect a shell in preparation for the impending invasion.

A large number of Canadian soldiers were issued bicycles for D-Day in order to quickly advance to the front and reinforce the men from the first wave. Privates Reg Martin, Rodney MacNeill, and George Banning load the bicycles onto an LCI (L) in preparation for the invasion.

Artillery is counted out in preparation for the bombardment of the Atlantic Wall just prior to the landings. Lieutenant/Bombardier Walter Cooper does the honours.

do training for quite a few years in what they call "gravel pits" or "chalk pits" over there and we'd go there in the morning and do these things and the whole purpose of that was to train us to make some forays into France. We knew that this was what we had to do in order to take the pressure off the Russian Front. We knew it was going to be a tough thing.

They kept talking about the "Atlantic Wall." We had no idea what the Atlantic Wall looked like. We sort of envisioned it being pillboxes from one end of France to the other, right through to Belgium. We knew our attack was going to happen. We had a pretty good O [Orders] group, and we were shown pictures in this camp maybe a week before.

John Turnbull, RCAF

We had all looked forward to the day when the invasion would start, and we wondered whether it could be successful. We had been bombing the communications, railways, and other centres more intensely about a month prior to the invasion. We didn't concentrate on any one spot. I suppose that was part of the philosophy: to make the enemy wonder just where it was all going to take place.

Ernie Jeans, 1st Canadian Parachute Battalion

Most of us were anxious to get going — I don't think we understood the enormity of what was happening. I think that's what most people felt: that we had had enough training, let's get going on whatever task we had to do and get it done.

Bob Dale, RCAF

The army in my way of thinking had a really tough time. They had those three years at least of waiting, and some more than that. I had a brother who was in the Toronto Scottish and he went over early — in '41 I guess — and was there the whole time. Training all that time with no action of any kind except Dieppe — it was pretty hard.

Cec Brown, RCAF

The night before D-Day Air Vice-Marshal Broadhurst, who was head of the 2nd Tactical Air Force, came down to give us a pep talk. And Johnny Johnson was at the next airfield with 144 Wing — he brought his men over too. Johnson and Broadhurst didn't have much respect for each other. Broadhurst greatly outranked Johnson, but Johnson was more popular than Broadhurst ever thought of being. So Broadhurst is making this pep talk and

D-Day brought together one of the largest fleets of aircraft ever assembled for one mission.

Two Canadian paratroopers dressed in full gear and prepared to load onto a C-47 Dakota for their trip to Normandy.

Paratroopers attending mass prior to leaving on D-Day.

he's boiling it down to this: "Fellows, this is the ultimate effort that we have to put in tomorrow. We can't afford to have anything happen jeopardize it, and I want you to go full out all the time. Give everything you can. I'm willing to sacrifice a Spitfire and a pilot for every ground objective you can destroy." Johnson spoke up: "Oh, beg pardon sir. Would you like to lead the first show and show by example of what you mean?" He said this so nicely that Broadhurst didn't have a comeback.

Aboard one of the ships in transit to Juno Beach, a soldier relaxes the men by playing the bagpipes.

Secrecy was of the utmost importance. Once the men went into their transit camps, there was no exit. The next time they would be able to move around freely would be in France.

Rolph Jackson, Queen's Own Rifles
You have to remember that we were young, irresponsible, and slowly growing up — but not normal growing up because we joined the army as kids and four years later we were at the beach.

Roy Clarke, RCAF
We were young men — I was twenty-one years of age. We were young, we were in good health, we had good minds, we were full of excitement, and to many of us the excitement was beyond anything else that we would ever see in the rest of our lives. I have never experienced anything like it and if I may say so, it was in one respect enjoyable to have this kind of excitement even though you had put your life on the line. But by the same token, we never thought that we would be knocked down. Death was all around us, you might say — especially when we

were on the bombing run — but we didn't dwell on it. We thought about it, but it didn't bother us.

The one thing that bothered us perhaps more than anything was after an operation when we came back to our sleeping quarters and there were empty beds and that question came up: Where are they? You didn't know if they'd been knocked down completely, you didn't know if they'd been knocked down and were in an escape position, you didn't know if they were knocked down and had been captured as a POW — you hoped that possibly that's what happened to them: they were knocked down, they bailed out, and they were captured prisoner of war and that they were alive. No operation was a piece of cake as some people tried to say it was — there was always something going on.

Richard Rohmer, RCAF

I'd just turned twenty. The feeling among the Mustang fighter reconnaissance pilots was one of euphoria: this was the day that we had all been looking forward to. It was the culmination of the effort that everyone had been putting in. We were told the day before to paint the black and white stripes on our airplanes — so we knew that D-Day was coming.

Bob Dale, RCAF

General E.H. Brown cleans a Browning machine gun atop a Sherman tank, preparing for the great crusade.

A newspaper article depicts the sort of antics that the paratroopers got up to awaiting the go signal. Each member shaved his head to create a letter. Together they spelled V-I-C-T-O-R-Y.

There was a tremendous feeling of elation and camaraderie of all the services, because I guess in a lot of people's minds for the first time in four years or so we could see hope and the thing ending and getting back home. I think of just the general excitement. When we came back from that detailed reconnaissance and arrived at the station, ground crew were just everywhere painting the planes. At that stage we knew the thing was on and I think "elation" is probably the best word. But there was also concern, because we all had a lot of friends and I had a brother — and we knew that they were all going to be involved in D-Day, or D plus one, two, three.

John Turnbull, RCAF

It had been stalled a day or so because of the bad weather and the bad forecasts, and when we got our final briefing and the little slip of encouragement came around over the signature of Eisenhower and whatnot, we were all very happy. "Okay, let's go. Let's support the fellas on the ground." Anything we could do in the air, we wanted to give them the support because we knew they needed it.

En route to Normandy, preparing to finally meet the enemy face to face.

D-DAY

HOUR
BY HOUR

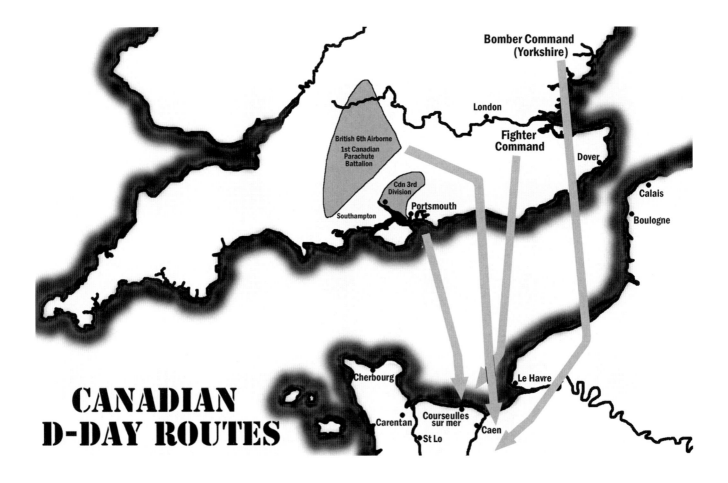

CANADIAN D-DAY ROUTES

D-Day began with most of the men en route to Normandy. The ships had been loaded up and had headed out late in the day on June 5. The bombers of the RCAF, RAF, and USAAF had been bombing sites all over Normandy throughout the night. They would continue to fly their missions until shortly before the landings. The aircraft carrying the airborne units had taken off during the night, some departing at 2200 hours, others later. The Canadian pathfinders who marked the drop zone (DZ) for the airborne were the first Canadians to set foot on French soil in the invasion, just minutes after midnight. They were soon joined by another 450 Canadian members of the airborne who parachuted in. For the 1st Canadian Parachute Battalion, it would be their first combat drop — and, in fact, the first ever use of vertical deployment in Canadian military history.

The paratroopers were also the first men to experience action on D-Day, landing during the initial hours of that day. Some landed in hot zones, others in the middle of fields without any resistance. Some splashed down in flooded areas. As the paratroopers landed, they sought to assemble their units and accomplish their missions before daylight. Their tasks were to eliminate gun emplacements that would threaten the landing beaches, destroy bridges that would be used by the Panzer units nearby during a counterattack, and hold the right flank.

Mark Lockyer, 1st Canadian Parachute Battalion
> I noticed on the flight over from England — as I looked down through the clouds and halfway across the English Channel — that there were so many boats from halfway across back to England that it seemed that you could almost jump from one ship to another and go back to the English coast. And it'd give you a great feeling that everybody was working for the same purpose.

Jan de Vries, 1st Canadian Parachute Battalion
> We went in these Albermarle bombers, and only ten men could go in each aircraft. They were converted to troop carriers and they also pulled gliders later.

A newspaper article pictures the first Canadians in France — the paratroopers who landed in the first few minutes of June 6, 1944.

In flight over the English Channel: the paratroopers travelled in Albermarle bombers, C-47 Dakotas, and Horsa gliders.

Left: Reconnaissance photo of Pegasus Bridge on the east flank of the invasion forces.

Top Right: Pegasus Bridge was a noteworthy objective of the British 6th Airborne, and it was the site of the first casualty of D-Day (a British paratrooper).

Bottom Right: Pegasus Bridge in 2003. It is now a monument to paratroopers, and it has an airborne museum right beside it.

You couldn't stand up in this thing. On the flight over I don't remember a lot — there was very little talk, as I recall. I remember just thinking, "Well, I wonder what's going to happen. I hope I do the job." I never thought about dying — I just thought about doing the job.

When we neared the coast we could see flashes of light through the porthole. Somebody said, "Oh-oh — we're over the coast and that's anti-aircraft fire."

When we crossed the coast it got really heavy and you could see a lot of these flashes through the portholes. We got through the worst of the barrage but the pilot was weaving all over the place and we were rolling around inside and cursing because he wasn't flying in a straight path.

He was taking evasive action and trying to avoid the heavy fire — we could see the odd tracer going up. I guess that's why so many guys got scattered all over the place. Some went straight in to the target, to the drop zone — at least they got onto the field. Others who got the evasive action — the pilots lost where they were supposed to be and when they saw a field that they thought looked familiar they'd just put on the green light and everybody would go out.

Ernie Jeans, 1st Canadian Parachute Battalion

I was in the medical section of the battalion — so I was in Headquarters Company. We left around midnight — or maybe shortly before — but around the midnight hour we took off for Normandy. Some of our battalion had left quite a bit earlier — C Company in the 1st Para Battalion was in the pathfinder — they actually went first of all the parachute brigades. We were under the understanding that it would be a sort of an uneventful flight.

Jan de Vries, 1st Canadian Parachute Battalion

Most of us went out about 1210. We were a little earlier than anticipated — I think we were supposed to go in at twelve-thirty and the rest of the battalion was to be in at one o'clock. It continued from then on and

The Canadian paratroopers made the leap into the pitch-black air (save for the anti-aircraft explosions) only to land off course, sometimes by many miles.

A newspaper covered the D-Day drop by the paratroopers with this photo, depicting the jump from an old bomber. Early waves flew on Albermarle bombers; later they were transported in C-47 Dakotas.

the whole division would be dropping in different fields. What they called the pathfinders and the ones who were to secure the DZ went in a half an hour early and I happened to be in the assault company who did that.

I remember when the doors opened there was a lot of light, because there were more flashes and bursts and more light came into the aircraft. We went out of the Albermarle bomber — a two-engine aircraft that was converted from a bomber because it really was too slow. The Albermarles were used very early on in the war, but the Germans were knocking them out — so they realized they were no good for bomb raids, and that's when they converted them to troop carriers. The second thought — the idea we heard was they wanted to fool the Germans that it wasn't paratroopers coming over — it was just another bombing raid.

The first 120 in our company went over in the Albermarle bombers. All the rest came out of the Dakotas — the American C-47, which held twenty-men sticks — and they could go out the door, which was faster. The red light came on and so the guys who were closest to the hole unhooked the door, raised them up, and hooked them on the sides of the aircraft so the hole was ready. After the first four men went out and they were gone — *zip*! — I don't know whether it was the next man or what, but somebody said the door's flopped and he got jammed in the half of the hole. Anyway they struggled and finally he disappeared and they re-hooked the door back up and the rest of us went out. But what had happened in the time that had elapsed, the last of us were dropped way the heck off where we were supposed to be. In my case there was no firing whatsoever — it was total darkness, I must have been seven miles away and there was no firing going on. I was looking for the ground — I remember it was black as the ace of spades and I couldn't see the ground at all. I thought, "It's got to be close here, I better get ready before I hit the ground" — but it caught me by surprise. Everything was all right — got out of my chute in a hurry, looked around — didn't recognize anything. Got out of the field over to a hedge and looked through. Just saw sort of a cart track and nothing else. I hadn't a clue where I was. I recognized nothing that we were supposed to because we had looked at maps and table models of the area — and there wasn't a thing that looked like that at all. So the orders were hit the rendezvous — if you're lost get back as soon as possible. I had no idea which direction to go but I heard the aircraft flying over so I thought, "Well they're coming from the coast so I'll walk in that direction." That turned out to be the right decision. There was some bombing going on over at the coast — I remember hearing that — but that was after I landed on the ground. I heard some walking towards the coast — I heard some rumbling. That was quite a distance away at that time.

Mark Lockyer, 1st Canadian Parachute Battalion

I was a private with the 1st Canadian Parachute Battalion having dropped into Normandy at about 1245 on the morning of June 6. Our job — when I say our job, this is 4 Platoon, B Company — was to demolish a bridge over the river Dives at the village of Robehomme. Coming in from the coast, we pretty well flew along the Dives River and when we got close to our objective, on would come the red light and then the green light and out we went. But the Germans had flooded wide areas to deny the invading troops an opportunity to use it. But anyway with paratroopers you just drop into the water and hope it's not too deep. As it panned out, the area that I dropped into was only about four, four and a half feet of water so I survived.

A massive airdrop delivers the paratroopers to France, to begin the liberation of Europe.

In order to defend Normandy, the Germans constructed dams to divert the rivers and flood the fields. These became deadly zones for paratroopers landing in the dark and weighed down with almost one hundred pounds of equipment.

Jan de Vries, 1st Canadian Parachute Battalion

The Germans had flooded the area all around the Dives River where we had to blow bridges. Those who landed in the fields — there was only three feet of water — they survived, those who landed in a ditch that would be six to seven feet deep with their loads — we lost a few men who happened to land in the water over those ditches — they just went straight down to the bottom and never got up again.

Mark Lockyer, 1st Canadian Parachute Battalion

I got out of my parachute, left it there, and looked around. I saw some trees off to the east a bit, and walked towards these trees because I figured they would be along the edge of the road. The end result was that having gone on the way to these trees, there were two fences that I had to get over and that was a difficult job when you're loaded down.

The sky was filled with parachutes between the Orne River and the Dives River.

Wilf Delaurie, 1st Canadian Parachute Battalion

In my case as far as I can remember we were deplaned around 1250. Well I was in the piat platoon. I was attached to B Company and our section was supposed to go up near the Dives River because that section of B Company was blowing a bridge and I was to give them protective fire from any tanks or any tank-type of vehicles in that location — but I never got there. We stood up and stood in the door and when we finally got the signal to go — possibly I think in our aircraft the signal could have come a bit late because none of us hit the actual drop site. That may have been a good thing because the drop zone did come under fire from artillery. When jumping you don't hesitate — you're going. You don't have time at the doorway to look — you're on the move, and you go out very quickly. In my case it was just fields, that's all I seen were fields. There was no fire at all in the area that I was. I landed by myself probably about three miles from the drop zone towards Caen, which would be about southeast of our actual drop zone. It took five hours to hook up with the battalion. First I tried to locate where the hell I was, which was very difficult. It was just farmland — there wasn't anything to go by.

As the grand Allied armada traversed the English Channel, it was an awe-inspiring sight for all who witnessed it. All told, there were 7,000 sea-going craft taking part in Operation Neptune. Canada supplied 108 vessels and 10,000 sailors to the fleet. Canadian naval craft cleared the sea lanes of mines, transported men and machinery for the invasion, and provided protection by keeping watch for submarines and E-Boats. The armed merchant cruisers *Prince Henry* and *Prince David* carried many of the Canadian troops across the Channel. A large number of men made the crossing on their landing craft.

Andrew Irwin, Royal Canadian Navy

Our objective when we set out from Portsmouth was to escort HMS *Hilary* over to the beaches together with the flotilla of Royal Marines who were in landing craft behind us.

Hilary was also carrying Major General Kellar, the commanding officer of the Canadian 3rd Division. At midnight we closed up action

HMCS *Algonquin* was one of seven thousand naval craft that participated in Operation Neptune (the naval component of Operation Overlord).

stations — that meant everybody had to go to their action station position — and we were following a channel that had been swept by the minesweeping flotilla. They left little blue lights on either side of the channel and so we were following these in.

A Canadian minesweeper off of the coast of Normandy. They moved in early to clear shipping lanes to the landing beaches.

While it was no real danger — we didn't think — from surface craft, there were mines floating around, and we saw several of those going by.

John Dionne, 17th Hussars

I was a driver of the jeep, and I had an officer, and a corporal, and another radio operator, I was also a radio operator. The four of us were in a jeep, and we got onto one of the barges, and we started crossing. We spent the night on the way over and in the morning we got to the beach.

Hal Whitten, Royal Canadian Navy

We weren't told where we were going — we didn't know until we got there. Just sent us out into the Channel to sweep with sonar for subs. It's indescribable, really — it's something you'd see in the movies but not believe. I was only a kid — I thought it was really exciting. I thought I was watching a war movie.

The weather was still inclement, with heavy clouds covering the moon and making it a very dark crossing. The seas were churning under the influence of high winds. Seasickness made many of the men feel wretched, and drained them of the energy that they would need so dearly when landing on the beaches that morning. The men would arrive for the invasion deprived of sleep, food, and any sense of good health.

Invasion craft en route to Juno Beach.

Doug Barrie, Highland Light Infantry

It was stormy and dark and the waves were quite rough but as you got further out into the Channel it got really rough. There was a lashing wind and dark clouds. The landing craft weren't that big and they just went every which direction — right to left, up and down. It was pretty hard to keep anything in and on an even keel! Once a few started getting sick, everybody got sick, it seemed.

There were forward and aft rooms down below deck, and of course the troops had to stay down most of the way across. The water was very, very rough — the Germans didn't expect us because of the rough sea. They didn't think that we could possibly do it. It ended up being a good decision to go because it started to clear up a bit. But we were tossed about like I don't know what, and being down below — it wasn't much fun.

They gave us buns and so on and what they call self-heating soup. The soup was in a can that you pulled the centre cap off, then lit the powder that was in there with a match and it burnt down and heated the centre of the can, and the soup around it would be heated by the time the powder burnt down to the bottom. It was very, very strong soup — had a lot of fat and so on in it. Hardly anybody could down it because of the rough seas. We were bringing up more than we were taking down. In fact we were issued with what they called vomit bags and I think each of us got three. Most of us could have used at least twelve.

The view from LCI (L) 306 of the flotilla, en route to Juno Beach.

Cooking a meal during the passage to Normandy, the men of the Highland Light Infantry on LCI (L) 306 would not enjoy the meal much due to the heavy seas. Few men were able to keep their meal down.

Landing craft crossing the English Channel. The men who made the crossing on these small craft recall vividly the terrible seasickness that gripped almost all of them.

Jack Martin, Queen's Own Rifles

Everybody was sick. Our platoon commander and his batman were on our craft and he had to run to the side, and he puked and lost all his false teeth and everything there. There was an awful lot of them getting sick because those little craft bounce around something terrible.

The Channel was filled with sea craft of almost every sort that night. From huge battleships to small landing craft, they were all there with a single purpose.

Doug Barrie, Highland Light Infantry

I think we were all awake, nobody could sleep. We were down below, we had to be down. I think it took about forty-six at the front and forty-six at the rear and I think there was another room — we were split up in three rooms on the boat. Luckily our room had what they call collapsible cots that came down, but there were only about fourteen inches between each cot and they were stacked four high, and they'd fold up. But they weren't being used. Our fellas couldn't use them because we found with all your kit and so on we couldn't squeeze in. We found that really we couldn't make use of them. With the tossing of the boat and everybody being sick and the smell and so on, it was hold on or else you might go flying. The floor was getting pretty greasy then. All you could think of was, "Let's get out of here as soon as we can, let's get it over with."

Catching a breath of fresh air up on deck of LCI (L) 306, the men of the Highland Light Infantry did not have much room to move due to the storage of their bicycles.

Jack Martin, Queen's Own Rifles

We did all our training in Scotland for the D-Day invasion. Every time we went on a boat I was deathly sick, so when we were on the craft going across on D-Day I told the seaman that I wasn't a very good sailor and that's why I joined the army. So he said, "Well, why don't you lie on the gunwale" — I was on an LCT landing craft tank —

LCI (L) 118 of the 2nd Canadian (262nd RN) Flotilla on course for Normandy, with a Dido-class cruiser in the background.

"and why don't you lay on the gunwale and look for mines on the way over." So I did. All night long I lay on the gunwale watching the water — never saw any mines. Over to our right in the middle of the night an aircraft came over and dropped flares and I was afraid we were going to be noticed.

Overhead the bombers of the RCAF made their way to strategic enemy targets: roads, bridges, railways, airfields, communications centres, and command posts. The members of the RCAF would be part of a monumental fleet of 171 Allied squadrons that would participate in D-Day. Bomber Command would drop thousands of tons of explosives, destroying German positions and slowing down their ability to counterattack the invasion forces as they landed on the beaches.

Roy Clarke, RCAF

The German flak guns were excellent, they were very accurate. They were mostly controlled by radar and the German radar was what I would call first class — it could direct flak guns or searchlights. And it's when you're coned in searchlights

An aircrew aboard an Allied bomber in cramped quarters.

that you're really scared, there's no question. The usual searchlights — there was one master beam, a blue-white beam in the centre surrounded by five or six white lights — and when they coned you, it was as bright as day. It is a frightening thing, the Germans used to hose flak up through the searchlight beam, and if you were at the end of that searchlight beam you were going to get hit, there was no question.

There were a lot of gun emplacements on that Normandy coastline. There were more up around the Calais area because that's the area they thought was going to be invaded. But all down the Normandy coast there were gun emplacements and there's no question they could make it pretty hot.

Ken Hill, RCAF

All across Yorkshire were scores and scores of airfields where the different planes of our Allied air force would be taking off and we would congregate in the sky and then cross the English Channel to our destination. That's where pretty well all your heavy bomber planes were located. At one time they said there were so many airfields in Yorkshire and in the northern part of England that one could walk from the east coast of England to the west coast of England without stepping off a tarmac. They were so closely nestled together.

Roy Clarke, RCAF

Bomber Command was in there to destroy as much of the industry as possible and stop Germany from bringing supplies towards the Normandy front where D-Day started. If we could stop supplies from being brought up by the Germans, then our Canadian and Allied armies could surge ahead and slowly work towards overtaking Germany. Bomber Command, whenever they could, would go out and soften up the German army that had previously been dug in at a certain location. This permitted our Canadian troops to proceed ahead. Each aircraft would carry upwards to twelve thousand pounds of bombs — the bomb would depend on the target that we were going to. When you put the Lancasters and the Halifaxes together carrying something like ten and twelve thousand pounds of bombs each, it's a total destruction of almost whatever they went after. There were less Allied troops lost in army fighting engagements simply because Bomber Command had already been through and softened up some of the army locations.

One thing that the German army did not predict or calculate was the actual D-Day landing in Normandy — our Canadians on Juno Beach, the British and the Americans on the other beaches. The actual landing point was a question mark for the German commanders. They thought that the landing would proceed a little further to the north at the location of the narrowest point of the English Channel. In order to keep the Germans guessing, Bomber Command sent over a number of raids prior to June the sixth, bombing targets, industrial targets and shoreline targets of the Germans north of the Normandy beachhead. The idea behind that was to give the Germans the impression that the Allies were preparing for an invasion at that location. It worked. The destruction by Bomber Command in that location was not that great, but it was enough to throw the Germans off their guard and to concentrate somewhere else. We hesitate to think of what would have happened if the German commander had have guessed that the Normandy beachhead was going to be the landing point and concentrated its troops through that area. It was bad enough as it was — but it would have been I think horrendous if they had have guessed. Fortunately and thank goodness they guessed wrong.

Explaining or even talking about what the odds were of survival of aircrew members on operations is tricky. There's a common theme that said one in four, maybe a quarter of all aircrews would not come back. In the Royal Canadian Air Force during the war, we lost just under ten thousand aircrews.

One hour into D-Day, Canadian ships were halfway across the English Channel. Briefings were over and the information was being disseminated amongst the men. The RCAF was in the midst of the bombing campaign: some planes were returning from their missions, some were delivering their payloads, some were on their way, and others were preparing to take off. The bombings would go on all night.

Many of the Canadian paratroopers were on the ground, heading for their rendezvous zones. Some encountered German patrols, but most were able to avoid them. A huge number were lost, or were so far off course that it would take them all night (and in some cases days) to arrive at their planned destinations. Some never made it and instead joined up with other units to accomplish their tasks. Such improvisation turned a potential failure into a success.

While many of the paratroopers got into the action early, others spent a lonely night in enemy territory, desperately searching for other Allied troops. Many were killed or wounded — the price that was paid for being in an elite company assigned to spearhead the invasion. Few men could boast of such bravery — being willing to jump out of an airplane behind enemy lines, armed only with what one person could carry. The glory bestowed on those who wore the maroon beret was well earned that night.

Ernie Jeans, 1st Canadian Parachute Battalion

We were told that most of the anti-aircraft material had been wiped out and that they had dropped decoys further up towards the Paris area. After a while when we hit the coast of France — it really got rocky — there were explosions and the plane was rocking back and forth. By the time we were ready to stand up to go, it was quite a rocky flight. I didn't know personally that there were going to be so many people coming on the ground — we had been briefed on our own particular tasks and I wasn't really that sure of the enormous amount of material and men that were coming.

Since I was in the medical section I really didn't concern myself too much about what the various companies were doing or what they were going to seize. We were more concerned about being able to set up in some sort of central place when we reached the rendezvous, and what would happen when we had enough wounded people there; where would we transport them to?

As we approached the drop zone, there was an announcement to stand up. The plane revved down quite a bit and we started to lose altitude because they wanted to

Left: Some paratroopers were captured by the Germans that night, as shown in this German photograph.

Right: Many paratroopers landed far from their unit members and spent a long time on their own, in the middle of enemy territory.

drop us as low as they possibly could. I happened to be number nineteen in the plane — there were twenty of us altogether — and another part of our medical section was at number twenty. As the plane started to rev down and as we approached the drop zone, somebody gave the order to go. I can remember that there was an air force person right at the door. We had so much equipment, he was helping us out and shoving people as they approached the door. Then what happened to me I don't think happened to anybody else. When I reached the door they stopped me from going out because they had gone over the drop zone — at least this is what the pilot said. Getting yourself worked up so that you're ready to go and then being told to go and sit down again was a little disturbing to say the least. So the two of us — nineteen and twenty — we sat down again and thought, "Well, this is a complete letdown — we're going to go back to England." But we didn't. The plane came around again and the two of us went out. The first eighteen in our plane left fifteen to twenty minutes before us and then we went around again and the two of us landed. It turned out to be very fortunate for me because the first eighteen landed were either captured or killed or missing or wounded.

Now the doctor — Dr. Brebner was his name — he was hurt during the landing and remained hidden for a while, but he was eventually captured. I talked to him after the war about how he survived the war in a prison camp — but I wasn't able to talk to any of the other people who were there. Whatever happened to them individually, I don't know.

We landed probably about one o'clock or one-thirty in the early morning of June the sixth. I got out of my harness and gathered up my equipment. I was in the centre of a farmer's field. I got out of the field and got to the side where there were hedgerows. I just stayed there for a moment until I got my wits about me to try to find out where I was — which I must admit was very, very difficult. I didn't have any idea where I was.

Mark Lockyer, 1st Canadian Parachute Battalion

Besides all our equipment — when I say equipment, that is rifle and bullets and gammon bombs and grenades — each one of us had a vest, which held twelve sticks of PHE — plastic high explosive. You had to collect up enough men with vests of plastic high explosives in order to demolish the bridge. On the way to the bridge, I got out of the river and onto the ground area where I collected up two or three of my buddies and headed towards what I thought was the bridge. I was lucky: I went in the right direction. I got to the bridge about ten after one, quarter after one, and we waited. There were other lads coming in with their loads of PHE and Captain Peter Griffin was there — that's our B Company second-in-command.

Wilf Delaurie, 1st Canadian Parachute Battalion

After about a half-hour I heard some small arms fire and I headed in that direction, figuring that we were the only ones in there, so it had to be some of our people who were involved in the firefight.

The third hour of D-Day found Canadian paratroopers on the ground. Some were searching for their units; others were preparing to attack their targets. The situation was tense: in the darkness of night, a shadow could be a friend, a foe, or merely a bush blowing in the wind.

Wilf Delaurie, 1st Canadian Parachute Battalion

I went for possibly an hour and I met up with two British airborne troops and they were pushing a six-pound anti-tank gun. They had landed in a glider that was totally wrecked. The jeep was totally wrecked but they managed to get the gun out. The two of them were hand-pushing this thing by themselves, so I gave them a hand and we finally came to a road and we figured, well, we'd have to push on the road, we weren't making any headway in the fields.

Jan de Vries, 1st Canadian Parachute Battalion

We heard then from the guys who had actually carried out all the objectives that had been assigned to us — blowing the bridge, taking out the German strongpoint, making sure that there were no Germans around the drop zone so that the rest of our troops could come in. All those jobs were carried out by thirty-five men who had landed on the field and headed to the rendezvous. The rendezvous itself was kind of a hooked edge, and they were to gather in that hook. So there were only the thirty-five with the major and one platoon officer and I think two or three NCOs. When the major

Aerial reconnaissance photograph of one of the paratroopers' objectives on D-Day.

realized that there didn't seem to be any more of his men coming — about an hour, hour and a half later — he decided that they'd better tackle that strongpoint, which was not too far away from the drop zones.

So they put in their attack and broke off a few guys to take the bridge. These men held that bridge until some engineers came along and set the dynamite up to blow the bridge. They also attacked the German headquarters in the village [Varaville]. The rest of the men went to the German strongpoint. That's where the major, the lieutenant, and four other men were killed.

The major had gone to the second floor of this gatehouse so they could overlook this German strongpoint. The Germans had machine guns around the strongpoint that they used to send out fire every once in a while. But their attention was on some of the other guys that were in a ditch close to the gatehouse who were firing at them to draw their attention away. The major told the guy with the piat gun — Corporal Oikle — to see if he could knock out or hit the concrete emplacement. At that time they didn't know there was a 75mm artillery piece in there. Oikle never could tell distance and the piat shell landed about fifteen feet short. He was being handed a second piat bomb when the German gun fired a high explosive shell into the room, which killed the major, Oikle, and the others. The men kept after that strongpoint and Dan Hartigan fired a 2-inch mortar shell — he was in a ditch at the time. Every once in a while the Germans would fire a burst over their heads but so long as they stayed low in that ditch they couldn't hit them. Dan got up just long enough to fire off the mortar bomb and on investigation later on they found out that he hit the breach of the gun and knocked out the sight and damaged it, so they never fired again.

Ernie Jeans, 1st Canadian Parachute Battalion

It was really a confusing situation. I don't think anyone ever imagined that by dropping at night that they would have so much confusion, and of course they didn't do it again. When we parachuted across the Rhine in March [1945], it was a daytime drop. When you did see people usually they were visible enough that you could tell from the uniforms and so on — I suppose you could make a mistake but fortunately I didn't.

Jan de Vries, 1st Canadian Parachute Battalion

The British 9th Battalion had the job to take out the Merville battery. They'd been planning this for months. They had a model, they made attacks and all that, and had a pretty good idea how they were going to handle it. Out of the 600 men that were trained for the job, only 180 some odd actually put in the attack. A Company from the

Canadians were to go to the right — that would be to the east side of them — and stop any German reinforcements from interfering with the attack. This was carried out successfully — not with all the A Company men, but they had enough to do the job. No Germans got through to interfere with the attack by the 9th British Battalion. When the Merville batteries were taken out and they had damaged the guns so they

Top Left: An overview of the Merville battery complex in 2003. On D-Day the site was surrounded by a trench system that had to be overcome before the artillery guns could be silenced.

Centre Left: Two bunkers of the Merville battery, a key objective of the British 6th Airborne, which included one company from the 1st Canadian Parachute Battalion. Severely undermanned, the paratroopers overcame the German position in the early hours of June 6.

Bottom Left: One of several concrete emplacements at the Merville battery. The guns were within striking distance of the British landing beach known as Sword, and they had to be silenced to ensure a successful invasion along the easternmost sector of the invasion.

Right: Aerial reconnaissance photograph of the Merville battery. The arrows indicate the position and direction of the advances on the targeted site.

couldn't fire them, they were to move to a preplanned defence line. A Company was to follow those men from the 9th Battalion that were left — now there weren't a lot of men, there was only about 60 I think left of the 180 some odd men. The A Company men followed and went to the same village where the 9th Battalion men dug in and when the 9th battalion was secure, the A Company men went up to Le Mesnil. That's where all our battalion men were to gather. That was our defence position.

Meanwhile, as the landing force moved closer to Normandy, the rough seas wreaked havoc with the men and the vessels. The flotilla strove to stay its course, as the positioning of the craft had to be maintained to ensure that every invasion unit was together and ready to strike at the same time. Splitting up would create a catastrophe at daylight, when the concentration of men at key landing sites was essential.

Jack Read, Royal Regina Rifles

As the time passed, we could hear the guns, see the ships, and it was very rough and very cold. Everybody was kind of hunkered down into whatever shelter they could get. Getting on to the wee hours of the morning, we began to see more and more and more of the aircraft overhead, and more ships behind us and beside us.

In the air, the RCAF continued to pound away at the German defences all over France. The attacks were scattered so that the actual landing sites would not be given away.

John Turnbull, RCAF

I'm pleased looking back that I and my crew were part of the D-Day operation. We flew into the gun emplacements north of Juno Beach at Houlgate, and in spite of the terrible weather that confronted us that night, my log book indicates that we bombed from nine thousand feet, which is quite low for Bomber Command people. We felt that we got our target and that we contributed to the D-Day operation by diverting attention to that area, immobilizing some of the artillery before our boys went in on the water.

Roy Clarke, RCAF

Each aircraft bombing was controlled by the navigator and his charting. The navigator plotted the course, the speed, and the direction right into the target, and the pilot went by these instructions. The bomb aimer — once he got into the target area — looked for identification through the track indicators, which were flares dropped by our pathfinder aircraft before the attacks started. Six Group Bomber Command sent out hundreds of aircraft, and each aircraft would follow through on these basic tactics approximately a minute and a half apart. There's no question that sometimes some were early and some were a little bit later, but all of those aircraft would drop a full load of bombs, which would cause a lot of destruction.

John Turnbull, RCAF

That was the twenty-ninth operation for my crew and I. We went in on the gun employment at Houlgate, which is near Cabourg in France. We had to fly from northern England — Yorkshire area. We had to fly the course of England and then branch over to it. Of course everything was radio silence. Going down the length of England would be a couple of hours at least.

There were two objectives, as I recall. One, of course, was to knock out the gun emplacements. The other was to confuse the Germans as to where the invasion was actually going to take place.

Roy Clarke (RCAF Bomber Command).

Roy Clarke, RCAF

All of us carried a little symbol of luck such as a rabbit's foot or something. Some fellas said that they wore the same pair of socks on every operation. Some fellas wouldn't shave before an operation, some fellas wore a scarf or a sweater. And there were fellas who carried something with them that they carried on the trip that they were on before because they came back. There was a certain belief that because I had this rabbit's foot with me the last trip, this rabbit's foot was bringing me good luck. I don't believe that anyone was ever afraid. If a person, if a crewmember was afraid, then he shouldn't be flying. Because if a person is afraid, they cannot do their job properly — and it's not just themselves that they are protecting. Remember we had seven members in that crew.

As a part of the invasion convoy, the HMS *Petunia* (K79) crosses the English Channel on D-Day.

As the night progressed, the Canadian paratroopers were completing their missions, despite being severely undermanned. Many still wandered the Norman countryside looking for their allies and their rendezvous zones.

Jan de Vries, 1st Canadian Parachute Battalion

B Company had to blow the bridge at Robehomme and stop any Germans. That was a major bridge that had to be blown because it could support German tanks very well. That was in the area of the flooded waters. But the engineers who were supposed to do the job hadn't arrived yet.

So there was Mark Lockyer and a British engineer who arrived on his own and the two of them gathered up explosives — each one of us was carrying an amount of dynamite — and it was all put together.

Mark Lockyer, 1st Canadian Parachute Battalion

By about three o'clock there were eighteen of us there and Captain Griffin says, "Does anyone know anything about how to blow this stuff up?" We were supposed to have a Royal Engineer to do the blowing job. He wasn't there and that's not unusual to get lost because there was a lot of country to wander over, and don't forget this is the dark of night and difficult to find your way around. I

Aerial reconnaissance photo of the bridge at Robehomme, an objective of the 1st Canadian Parachute Battalion.

Wreckage of a bridge destroyed by Canadian paratroopers on D-Day.

said to Captain Griffin, "I know a little bit about explosives." I had taken a course at Wainwright, Alberta — a demolition course — and had been instructing about demolitions for a little while before I left for England. "Well," he says, "you better get at it then."

There were two I-beams under the bridge, and somebody had to stand on my ankles so that I didn't fall into the river Dives as I reached underneath and put the plastic high explosives on the bridge. When I had that done, I collected up some people's gammon bombs and thirty-six grenades to make more explosives and put them all together, tied them to the I-beam, and then backed off with a little electrical gizmo that sets her alight. I told everybody to clear off, and at 0320 I blew it.

It wasn't completely blown, but nobody could drive a tank or a car or a jeep or anything else over it because it was dipping in the water. We just guarded it and kept everybody off it until about six o'clock — the Royal Engineers came along with much more explosives and they finished the job.

Jan de Vries, 1st Canadian Parachute Battalion

The next thing that happened was the Germans' infantry arrived in trucks and a bit of a battle took place. They shot up the first truckload and got most of those, and the second truck backed up and got out of the way and went around the bend and started firing some mortars.

The men aboard the ships passed the time writing letters home, playing cards, or immersing themselves deep in thought. At 0330 breakfast was served, with the men being treated to bacon and eggs on some of the larger ships. Unfortunately, seasickness prevented many from eating that morning, and those who did manage a few bites were unable to keep their food down.

**Doug Barrie, Highland
Light Infantry**

We all got letters off home to let the family know that we were in good shape — we couldn't say anything about D-Day or anything, but I think the general public had a pretty good idea that it was coming soon. We'd been all equipped at the camp beforehand with our battle dress that had been gas impregnated in case the Germans used gas. It smelt terrible and the battle dress was very hot because it filled up a lot of the weave. We had our helmets, we had our D-Day boots, we had everything that we needed. Three of the companies were carrying the bikes and one company was to be carried on the carriers — that was D Company, the company which I was with. I had 16 Platoon and we were fortunate we didn't have the bikes. One of the reasons for that was the fact that they could only load so many bikes onto these landing craft with all the crew.

During the hours en route to Normandy, many men spent their time writing letters to family and friends. Company Sergeant-Major D.D. Perkins writes home during his trip on an LST.

Food was served to the men in the early hours of the morning on the larger ships and landing craft.

For many of the men, the rough seas erased any chance of enjoying a hearty meal before combat.

Rolph Jackson, Queen's Own Rifles

It was my turn — we ate actually mess navy style and I went out — my turn to draw rations for our table — about three-thirty, four o'clock. I have to go up on deck to get to the galley to draw rations. We could see the outline of the flotilla and that's all you could see — ships all over the place — literally hundreds … big ships, small ones, large landing craft, landing ship tanks …

In the air, the RCAF continued to pound German-occupied France. Only anti-aircraft batteries endangered the flights, as the Allies maintained air supremacy. The Luftwaffe was no longer the formidable power that it had once been.

John Turnbull, RCAF

I recall going across the English Channel and the navigator had his G-box and radar and my crew was under orders of silence all the time unless there was something that had to be said. Suddenly over the intercom came the words, "My God they've got a whole brand new island down there!" He was talking about all the invasion ships that were going across, not only Juno Beach, but also to the other beaches on Normandy. Oh it was really something. From the pilot's seat I couldn't see it, but he was down and in front.

Richard Rohmer, RCAF

We got up at three in the morning to be briefed by the intelligence people and by our wing commander, and we couldn't have been more pleased. The objective for my squadron — we were fighter reconnaissance — was to do low-level visual reconnaissance to see what was on the ground and then to report that to the army. Ultimately we were to do low-level photography of locations that the army wanted photographed in enemy territory. We were also assigned to do artillery direction.

On D-Day the specific role that I took part in was to do a low-level visual reconnaissance of the city called Caen, and then come back over the beaches and do a patrol and reconnaissance and a defensive action if necessary over the beach. And that's exactly what we did.

Roy Clarke, RCAF

A tour of operations at that particular time in Bomber Command was thirty operational trips over France and Germany. Some aircrews were knocked down on their first operation, some after three or four operations. Some aircraft caught it on their last operation. I flew in our squadron alongside many very experienced crews, just like us, knocked down on twenty-fifth, twenty-sixth, twenty-seventh trip and there is no explanation as to why. There is no real knowing when you are going to catch a packet. Even though we were well trained, there certainly was a lot of luck.

John Turnbull, RCAF

There was a bit of a buzz and conversation and I can remember the rear gunner, who was from Saskatchewan, he said, "I'm bending my turret and my guns to take a look and all I can see is black down there." We'd go in in waves, we had three minutes to be in and off the target. We had been flying for quite a while and so the last ten to fifteen minutes or so the bomb aimer pretty well took over the instruction of the aircraft to go into the target. He would be calling the shot — we didn't reduce height. The last minute or two you got specific instructions of left-left, right adjustment, left-right, and all the time the other boys are keeping their eyes open for converging aircraft at that same height. Occasionally you looked up and there was a Lancaster or a Halifax above you with his bomb bays open and you wondered whether they were going to press the button at that time.

Roy Clarke, RCAF

On just about every operation the aircraft would get peppered; it's like throwing a handful of gravel on a tin roof. This was spent flak — in other words the flak shell exploding and portions of it knocking up against your aircraft and causing a bit of a clatter! You knew you were getting peppered, but you cannot fly through to a target and fly through a flak barrage without getting peppered. Every aircraft came back from an operation at some time or other with holes. Fortunately for the aircraft and their crew the holes were in the right place. Sometimes a stray piece of flak could get into an engine and knock it out, or cause a fire. The Lancaster and the Halifax could fly on three engines at any time. They could not get up to the same height as other aircraft, but they could still carry on on three engines.

John Turnbull, RCAF

We had to go in using the G-box, the radar boxes, as much as we could, lining up with the character of the coastline and then switching at the very last minute to follow the bomb aimer's instructions. At the very last minute he called for severe turn and hopefully the bombs did some damage when they got down there. We bombed gun emplacements and we were not told of Juno Beach or any of the invasion plans. What we got is a message saying: "Do a good job, fellas."

Daylight began to reveal outlines and details around 0400 hours. The armada was more than dark outlines in the ocean, and in the distance flashes could be seen. To the east the flashes came from the RAF bombing of Le Havre. To the west, they were from the German flares at Utah and Omaha beaches. The Americans had been spotted.

The Canadian 3rd Division continued towards its destiny, and the small landing craft were lowered into the sea, preparing to embark on the great crusade.

Doug Barrie, Highland Light Infantry

At first light, some of us were allowed up on deck. We had to take turns because there wasn't much room. The inner part of the craft was full of the bikes. There were just the outer edges, so a few at a time would go up there and try and smell a little fresh air and try and feel a little better.

Jack Read, Royal Regina Rifles

I commanded a group of our men on board a landing craft tank, a landing craft with Bren gun carriers that I was the section commander of. Accompanying us was some artillery people, either the 12th or 13th Field, who were also on board. I had been given a satchel with information before we left England. At a certain hour we were supposed to open this information, which I did, and briefed the men on board about what we were doing and where we were going. Not knowing exactly where we were going — they didn't tell us any information that we were going to any particular place, but that it was in France.

LCI (L) 299 carrying members of the 9th Infantry Brigade across the English Channel.

Above: Dawn broke early as the Allies were operating on double daylight savings time.

Top Right: View from HMCS *Prince David* of large landing craft in the rough seas carrying tanks, men, and material to Juno Beach.

Bottom Right: Captain A. Mendelsohn goes over the plans with his men, with details that had been top secret until that morning.

Doug Barrie, Highland Light Infantry

It was quite an amazing sight to see all the many, many hundreds of craft that were all going in the same direction.

A lot of them had these balloons attached to them — the landing craft didn't, but the larger boats that carried vehicles and so on did. The balloons were on the winch from the boat. They were up so that if the German aircraft attacked the balloon would tend to either entrap them or steer them off

from attacking. As far as I know I don't remember there being any in our area attacked by enemy aircraft on the way over. I think it was a complete surprise.

Left: Convoy of landing craft headed for Normandy.

Right: Barrage balloons were attached to larger ships to inhibit strafing and bombing raids by German aircraft. For the most part, the Luftwaffe never showed up on D-Day.

The air force bombers continued their bombing and reconnaissance missions, and also employed some deception to confuse the Germans.

Ken Hill, RCAF

We had Sterling bombers that were flying back and forth over the English Channel and they were dropping tinsel in what was called a nickel raid — they'd be dropping tinsel down so that the enemy radar screen would be just blipped out and they would think that there were thousands and thousands of aircraft there, when actually there weren't any.

Meanwhile, paratroopers on the ground organized and prepared to head towards their objectives.

Jan de Vries, 1st Canadian Parachute Battalion

It started to get daylight around four o'clock, so you could actually make out movement down the field. I could see where I'm going along this hedge. I saw some movement ahead of me and I watched it coming and I thought, "Geez, they look like my guys from our outfit." So I gave a whistle and they turned and they had their weapons ready. I don't know what I said, but they recognized me and the four of us got together and then we carried on.

Captain Kelly of HMCS *Prince David* briefs the men about the D-Day operations. All across the fleet the final plans were divulged.

Two gliders in a French field. The Allies did not account for the hedgerows when planning for landing areas for the Horsa gliders. Many crashed, as there was little space to land in the Norman fields.

We came along this field and there were gliders landing. I clearly remember two gliders. One was coming in for a landing and straightened out. About a hundred feet up another one came over and the two collided. Jesus, there was guys tumbling out of the air, most of them were killed landing on the ground. What a hell of a sight that was.

We knew the general direction where our battalion was supposed to be. We headed there and went down this ditch where there was a little stream. The commandos were supposed to be in that area, so they must have run into some Germans because there was one dead. We crossed that creek and carried on.

As dawn broke in Normandy, the weather had not yet cleared up. The northwest winds blew at fifteen knots, and the water was unusually choppy, with metre-high waves (in good weather the waters are calm, with practically no waves). Typically the water creeps up the tidal flat and barely laps the shore as the tide comes in. Not so on D-Day. The bad weather of the previous few days had churned the seas and made the marine conditions less than perfect. The weather would gradually improve, but the rough waters would not calm down in time for the landings.

Aboard the armada of Allied ships, everyone went to their action stations. The entire invasion force was prepared to engage the enemy.

0500

Jim Parks, Royal Winnipeg Rifles

It was pretty rough at that time because we were out in the open sea. We were in a landing craft tank, and we had two armoured bulldozers in front that belonged to the 6th Field Engineer Regiment. There were the sappers with them, and we had two sections of mortars, which meant that each section had two carriers with a trailer behind one of them to carry extra ammo and extra rations. The rations were supposed to be good for two weeks.

At sea it was rough. They gave us seasickness pills, and I was one of the

LCI (L) 118 of the 2nd Canadian (262nd RN) Flotilla, carrying personnel of the 9th Infantry Brigade en route to France on D-Day.

Men of Le Régiment de la Chaudière aboard an LCA alongside HMCS *Prince David*, offshore from Bernières-sur-Mer.

Members of the Canadian Scottish Regiment aboard an LCA alongside HMCS *Prince Henry*.

three lucky ones who didn't feel that bad. I popped a few in and round about daylight they passed out little bottles of rum. Not many people could have it so I was put in charge to fill the water bottle up with the rum that wasn't drunk in case we needed it later on for medicinal purposes or something like that.

For some of the paratroopers operating behind enemy lines, the immediate challenge was not combat, but getting to where they were going.

Wilf Delaurie, 1st Canadian Parachute Battalion

We pushed the artillery gun for another two to three hours before we met up with a couple of my troops, who turned out to be a 1st Canadian Parachute Battalion column heading for what we called the "brickworks" or the "crossroad" or Le Mesnil. That would be five to five-thirty in the morning at least, so I never did get to where I was supposed to. It was three or four miles in the other direction. I was possibly going to set out for the river Dives and they said, "Well, there's no point in it now," and I believe

View from HMCS *Prince David* shortly after dawn on D-Day. A minesweeper and infantry landing craft can be seen in the distance.

at that time the bridge had already been blown. The drop was so wide-spread that they sent their troops here, there, and everywhere and this is why we were very badly scattered. The resistance at that time was nil in that particular area. Now lots of other of our battalion met resistance, but not in the particular area where we were.

RCAF planes continued to take off from England and make their way across the English Channel to begin their missions.

Richard Rohmer, RCAF

When we got up we were fed a huge breakfast by our favourite cook, Stradioti, at our 39 Reconnaissance Wing kitchen. We were airborne in our Mustang fighters at dawn that morning, at the assigned time — two of us, Jack Taylor and myself — to do our particular reconnaissance. The feeling was one of high euphoria: we were really keen to go. It was the most exciting day that we ever thought could happen.

It was light, though the sun was obscured by a high overcast — probably about ten or eleven thousand feet. Below, the waves were intense on the water, but the whole sector, all the way across from Portsmouth and Southampton, was covered with ships, boats — vehicles of every kind. The impression made by the number of ships was just incredible in that ninety-mile passage across to Normandy.

View from LCI (L) 306 of the assault landing on Nan White beach at Bernières-sur-Mer.

As the grey daylight got brighter, the Normandy coast was visible to all of the ships, and details could be made out. At the same time, however, the Germans could also see the massive armada heading towards Normandy, and the guessing was over. They now knew where the landings were going to take place.

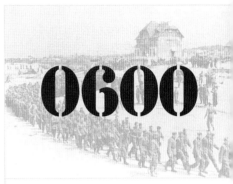

The German defenders began sending reports back to headquarters, with varying degrees of success. In many areas the lines of communication had been sabotaged by the French Resistance and the paratroopers. But even those communications that did get through were of little help: the German troops along the Normandy sector of the Atlantic Wall had less than two hours to prepare for the onslaught that was heading their way.

Shortly after 0600 hours, the naval bombardment commenced, hammering the emplacements along the coastline as well as the large artillery bunkers that were situated further inland. To reach these bunkers, the Allied Navy battleships and cruisers unleashed their 16-inch guns. Off the coast of Juno Beach, HMCS *Diadem* targeted the German battery that was positioned inland at Beny-sur-Mer, while HMCS *Belfast* set its sights on the Ver battery behind Gold Beach as well as some positions behind Juno.

At 0610 hours the destroyers unleashed their fury on the targets along the Juno Beach coast. *Kempenfelt, Faulknor, Venus, Fury, Vigilant, Bleasdale, Algonquin, Glaisdale, Sioux, Stevenstone,* and *La Combattante* battered all of the emplacements in an attempt to destroy them before the landings on the beaches took place. But the Allies had not anticipated the construction of the German bunkers and pillboxes. They were concrete reinforced with metal and were several feet thick. Unless there were direct hits on gun openings, the massive shells that the Allies were firing at the emplacements were causing only dents. Inside, the German troops were suffering from concussion and hearing loss, but they were still alive and could fire guns. After D-Day, the navy found that the naval bombardment was successful in knocking out only 14 percent of the German fortifications.

Andrew Irwin, Royal Canadian Navy

As we moved slowly in towards the beach, HMS *Rodney*, which was one of the Royal Navy battleships, was behind us, and at about six o'clock they started pushing in their heavy armament, which was 16-inch shells. They could go twenty and twenty-five miles with those things. It was quite awesome to see those floating over your head. At the same time the air force were flying over us and I have never seen so

Left: View from LCI (L) 306 of the naval armada on D-Day.

Right: HMS *Llangibby Castle* and other landing craft as viewed from LCI (L) 306 on D-Day.

many planes at one time since. They actually put a cloud over when they went by — they blacked out the sky.

We saw the paratroopers coming dropping in. It's quite something when you're sitting there and watching some guys get picked off as they're coming down.

Private Jack Roy of Le Régiment de la Chaudière preparing to disembark from HMCS *Prince David* for Bernières-sur-Mer.

Jack Read, Royal Regina Rifles

As we approached we could see the explosions from the bombing and the shelling from the various different kinds of armament that were being used to supposedly soften up the land so that we wouldn't have too much to fight against.

Jack Martin, Queen's Own Rifles

When those big naval guns let blast — wow! You sure wondered what was going on there when those 16-inch guns fired. The shells landed well inside the coast. There was a hell of a lot of noise — I had my ears blasted out.

In addition to naval shelling of the German emplacements from the sea, the air force was intensifying its bomb runs along the coastal fortifications and other strategic sites inland.

So great was the combined bombardment from the air and the sea that return fire from Juno Beach was contained. The defenders were not about to come out during this rain of destruction.

Jack Martin, Queen's Own Rifles

We could hear the aircraft droning all the time. Fantastic. I never ever, ever dreamt that they could put so many craft into the water. Where were they all the time we were in England? We were there three and a half to four years and we'd never seen those landing craft all around.

John Turnbull, RCAF

We were back on the ground by six or six-thirty, I suppose. We landed, taxied in, shut down, went back in to the dispersal point, signed the aircraft off, made notes as to things that weren't quite right so that they could be fixed up. Then we went into debriefing. The intelligence people debriefed us with all the questions that they had to ask to determine just how successful that trip had been. The gunnery leader talked to the gunners, the navigator leader, and whatnot, and then they talked to the crew as a unit. There were seven members in a bomber crew. Usually they had a toddy of rum to sort of warm you up — I and the crew very seldom took that.

It was an hour before we were into the mess hall having a bit of breakfast. Breakfast for aircrew was usually bacon and eggs and this kind of thing. We were the only ones who got pampered that way, and we were also pampered by having sheets and blankets. Then we went to bed, crawled into bed hoping that we didn't have to fly the next night.

At 0630, the Allies' radio silence was broken, and the airwaves crackled with communications and commands. The Germans knew the attack was coming, and they could no longer do anything to prepare for the assault; it was no longer necessary to keep it secret. The command went out to commence loading the men into the landing craft from the larger ships.

Four artillery regiments were loaded in twenty-four LCTs, and as they lined up offshore, they began their own barrage on the Juno Beach targets. Ninety-six 105mm cannons pounded the German positions. The 12th Field Regiment focused on a German position in Courseulles-sur-Mer, while the 13th Field Regiment fired on a position just west of the cliff. The bombardment did not destroy the emplacements, but it did stop the Germans from preparing for their defence.

Ready to leave HMCS *Prince David*, members of Le Régiment de la Chaudière head across the main deck for the landing craft. Destination: Bernières-sur-Mer.

Jack Martin, Queen's Own Rifles

When dawn broke I could see a vague outline of the land. Then we got closer and closer and I thought, "I have never seen so many craft in the water." Then finally they told me to get down and as soon as I got down from the gunwale the rockets started firing over our heads to the land, where it was all smoke at that time.

Ed Reeve, Armoured Corp HQ

We were on a big landing barge. It was scary, because I couldn't swim, and I had big boots on and everything. I wondered how I was going to get on this thing without falling in the water. It was moving all over the place.

Joe Oggy, Queen's Own Rifles

From the big ship they had a big scrambling net with big squares in it and you got to scramble down there to get into the landing craft. I was the last one to get in there — in fact I almost fell in because the waves were coming up and I went to step in and the boat was down — it was lucky I was hanging on.

From that big ship we got down into the little one and then we went in. We had our equipment and everything else. I carried a Sten gun, which I loved, while the rest of my men carried rifles. Those rifles were terrible: single shots *bang-bang,* instead of like the ones the Americans had, which you could cock once and then *bang-bang-bang-bang-bang.* This is one of the few things that I hold against our country — not being smart enough to realize that we needed good weapons.

Troops aboard HMCS *Prince David* prepare to go ashore. They were positioned just offshore from Bernières-sur-Mer.

Troops on board HMCS *Prince David* wait for their turn to go ashore and fulfill their duties of the day.

Lowering a loaded LCA into the sea from HMCS *Prince Henry*.

Frank Ryan, North Shore (NB) Regiment

We came across on an LSI — landing ship infantry. Kind of like a freighter, maybe a little bit bigger. The LCAs were slung along the sides of the ship. And what we would do when they had dropped anchor — they lowered us into the water and it was pretty heavy seas — a little bit tricky, and we just moved away from the landing ship, the LSI, and circled there until it was all organized.

Rolph Jackson, Queen's Own Rifles

For some unknown reason, but likely we were ahead of schedule, they pulled us around in a great big circle, and when we did come in daylight was pretty well on.

August Herchenratter, Highland Light Infantry

Some of the landing craft were hit before that because they had those 88s — the big guns up there — and they just shot down on the battleships that were in behind us. Then it took quite a long time for all those ships. Landing craft had to get out and get in a row.

Joe Oggy, Queen's Own Rifles

That was early in the morning, between six and seven o'clock. They gave us little bags, like Simpsons or Eaton's bags, to bring our breakfast up in, which a lot of men did.

On our way in one man went bonkers and tried to get over the side and we had to grab him and pull him back in again. He was the only one who tried to get out and from then on we just went right in.

Francis Godon, Royal Winnipeg Rifles

First they give us a mug of rum. That made you want to go get them, guy. Just before we got on the landing craft our commanding officer said, "Well, you must remember. You guys are fighters and you go up there and get them, but I don't think none of you guys will be coming home." We told him, "We're all coming home, we're going to go in there and kick butts."

With key tasks already accomplished, the paratroopers moved on to other assignments. The troops offshore were ready to attack, and it was crucial that the Germans be prevented from sending in reinforcements.

Jan de Vries, 1st Canadian Parachute Battalion

The engineers arrived at Robehomme and blew the rest of the bridge up and cratered both approaches so that they were totally impassable to any German tanks. The troops from the bridge were then called to the village of Robehomme — it was on the high ground — where they set up machine guns to cover the bridge near the area in case any more German troops arrived.

Weary paratroopers take cover in a crater. Most had not slept since the night of June 4/5.

Wilf Delaurie, 1st Canadian Parachute Battalion

There weren't too many of the Germans at Le Mesnil at that time. They were intermittent. They stopped and I don't really know if we had any German patrols come through in the night or not. The mortar fire was very heavy the next day and for the next few days. We weren't there very long before we were digging. I think one mortar shell urges you to dig very hurriedly. We were in a holding situation. We were to protect that flank so that the Germans couldn't get reinforcements down to the beachhead.

Paratroopers going over plans. Due to being widely scattered on their drop into Normandy, the 1st Canadian Parachute Battalion had to tackle their missions while severely undermanned.

Ernie Jeans, 1st Canadian Parachute Battalion
By that time we had consolidated around our rendezvous point at the brickworks near the village of Le Mesnil. Some of the officers and the colonel and so on were there. We had quite a bit of equipment with us. There wasn't too much actual fighting at that time. There was some — you could hear some roaring in the distance and so on — but to be suddenly attacked by a group of people ... that didn't happen.

When I arrived I was trying to find out where the commanding officer was so that I could report to him and tell him where we were going to set up. Of course at that time I had no realization that the doctor and some of my other buddies that were in the medical unit had in a sense disappeared.

All of the Allied landing craft were now lined up and in place. They were just offshore, and ready to invade Fortress Europa. In less than an hour all of the well-laid plans would give way to the reality of battle.

As the landing craft started to move in, the artillery and the tanks bombarded the shoreline to continue softening the resistance at the landing site. The larger landing craft carried 4.7-inch rounds, while each smaller landing craft had a multiple rocket launcher that fired salvos towards the beaches. The hope was that if the explosions didn't knock out the emplacements, at least they would create craters that would give the men some cover going in.

The plans called for the bombardment to continue until just a few minutes prior to the landings on the beaches. However, due to the rough seas and the strong cross-current of the tide, the craft were so unevenly positioned when the barrage was discontinued at approximately 0730 (the time varied along the beach) that there was a gap of fifteen to forty-two minutes before the troops landed on the beaches. The barrage ended early for fear that any rounds falling short of their targets would kill Canadian troops. This gave the German defenders a great deal of time to prepare and to man all of their guns.

Andrew Irwin, Royal Canadian Navy

Hilary peeled off to go to its station and we went inshore to do our bombardment. We were right off of Juno Beach — Courseulles-sur-Mer. If I recall correctly we took out some gun placements and there were several houses and other buildings that were our particular target. So we were bombarding from seven until just before H-Hour, when the troops were supposed to hit the beach, and we had to be stopped bombarding before that.

Canadian landing craft race ashore to face the Germans head-on.

View of the shoreline at Juno Beach for the men in the first wave.

Though the naval bombardment stopped firing on the coastal fortifications, inland sites remained targets. The air force, meanwhile, continued its assault on the inland.

Richard Rohmer, RCAF

We did our reconnaissance to Caen and then came back up the Orne River. We went over a place called Ranville, and at Ranville there's a bridge, now called Pegasus Bridge, which is the very famous location where the British came in with their Horsa gliders, landed in the fields just to the southeast of the bridge, did the big battle, and then took it. Here we were coming up the Orne River and saw these two huge gliders sitting in the fields next to this bridge — that was quite a sight.

Cec Brown, RCAF

I probably took off about 0730 and we'd be sure to be there by 0800. There were so many ships and they were so tightly lined up you'd think you could land on them — they were solid. A few of them got a little overzealous and started firing at us, but they didn't knock any of us down — at least not on our wing. It was just a breathtaking sight, to see how many were going in.

I was on the first show in my Spitfire. We got out over there about eight o'clock and patrolled Juno and Sword beaches, which were side by side. We patrolled for an hour and then we were relieved and went back again. We had two teams in each squadron. The second team patrolled twelve o'clock 'til one and then we went back at four o'clock for another hour and the other team went back at eight o'clock. They doubled British summertime at that time and it was still broad daylight at eight o'clock at night. So all together we had four trips over to Juno and Sword beaches in a Spit IX. The Spit IX gave you a lot of confidence: we felt it was the best damn airplane around. It was very manoeuvrable, very easy to control, and it just had no vices — it never surprised you with any unexpected movements at all. And you felt part of it.

Jim Parks, Royal Winnipeg Rifles

We saw on the way in two Spitfires going along, strafing the beach. I think somebody said one got hit further on by one of our own — there was so many shells firing and stuff coming in, he said it got hit by our own shells.

Only the field artillery units continued to fire on the German emplacements during the final approach to the beaches. At 0739 the 19th Field Artillery pummelled the fortifications at St. Aubin-sur-Mer, and at 0744 the 14th Field Artillery did the same at Bernières-sur-Mer. The field artillery units would continue to fire over the heads of the landing troops for the next half-hour, giving them the only close-in support that they could expect.

Arthur John Allin, 14th Field Regiment

Going over and approaching Normandy the seas were fairly rough and a lot of the men were seasick. When we approached the shore there were thousands of ships, which we couldn't see, but we knew that there were a lot of them there. The battleships and everything were there. The guns were firing onto the shore to soften up the enemy.

Our particular unit was the 14th Field Regiment, and we used self-propelled guns with 105mm guns on board. We were just like a tank with the top taken off so that we could fire the gun and we were pretty well loaded with our own equipment, plus we took in equipment and arms for the infantry.

Jim Parks, Royal Winnipeg Rifles

One funny thing, I remember this, the first carrier that went off was this fellow — we used to call him "String Bean" Whitey. He was from St. Thomas, Saskatchewan. He was hanging on to this compo box and he was trying to grab it and as he's grabbing it, it's spinning around in the water — he couldn't get a full grip on it. It was carrying him from right to left. Apparently he was picked up by the navy. He was a good eater and the joke was the first thing he'd do is head for the mess deck.

Left: View facing east along the shoreline at Courseulles-sur-Mer, 2003.

Right: A Canadian Churchill tank serves as a monument by the beach near Graye-sur-Mer, 2003.

Douglas Lavoie, Fort Garry Horse

In the assault wave that landed at Juno Beach there were two squadrons from the Fort Garry Horse and two squadrons from the 1st Hussars. There were twenty tanks in a squadron, so that would comprise a total of eighty tanks in that wave. The 1st Hussars were from London, Ontario, and the Fort Garrys were from Winnipeg. We supported the different infantry regiments. C Squadron — of which I was a member and a driver of one of the tanks — we supported the North Shores from New Brunswick.

Due to the heavy seas, the DD tanks of the 1st Hussars were unloaded closer to the shore than originally planned. The original plan was to have the tanks arrive onshore in advance of the artillery. This would provide two advantages: first, the tanks' large-calibre cannons could be used to eliminate the remaining German emplacements, and second, the tanks would give the incoming infantrymen some cover. But when the tanks entered the water one thousand yards off of Mike Sector they struggled in the waves. Many capsized, some sank, and only fourteen made it to shore. Few would arrive at the beaches ahead of the landing craft, leaving most of the men to face artillery with only rifles and grenades.

The results of the deployment of the DD tanks were so poor in Mike Sector that it was immediately decided that the DD tanks headed for Nan Sector would be unloaded right on the beach. This would spell catastrophe for the men landing there, since they would be landing before the tanks as well.

Philip John Cockburn, 1st Hussars

There were six tanks on the craft, and we just sat around looking wise. There were no such things as beds; we were there and they weren't going to take us off, so we just leaned up against the tank and went to sleep. There was nothing to do, just nothing to do. When we did get going — we were one of two squadrons of DD tanks going off at the same time — they got us off a way too far out. My tank alone got to shore; the other ones weren't so lucky. The duplex drive tank had two propellers on the back, as well as thirty-two air pillars. And there were ten hydraulic struts that held the tank up with the false decking around the outside of the tank. In rough water, when the waves hit, the struts would collapse. And the tank goes on down. Along with the men too.

Trucks and tanks were transported aboard LSTs on D-Day.

There were four or five or six of a crew on each craft, with six tanks. When you were unloading, the door at the back would come right down like a big open mouth at the tail end of this thing. There were big chains on either side, and the door went down at about a seventy-five-degree angle, and when they hollered "Down door," it went down. There would be one tank sitting halfway up on that door so they couldn't just shout right away — they had to warn you. And that's what they did. They warned us, but that didn't help matters at all [in preparing for the rough seas].

Tanks being transported through the rough waters towards the beaches.

Douglas Lavoie, Fort Garry Horse

Being on the landing craft tanks going in — what everybody talks about is the terrific noise and the bombardment going on by the navy at the same time, and the air force flying over and strafing and bombing. Most of us — well I know on our landing craft — we'd be quite a ways out by this time, and we were all standing there on top of our tanks where we could see over the rim of the LCT. Smoke and bombing and the explosions going on. Some of the regiments of the DD tanks let their tanks out way too far out. I don't know about the squadrons of the 1st Hussars, but I know that one of them they lost at least half their tanks before they even got to shore. Not from the enemy fire, but just from the horrendous waves.

Engineer units were the first to hit the shore, mere minutes before the first wave. Their mission was to clear the beaches of mines and obstacles and create a safe path for the landing craft to come in on. They faced intense gunfire, as the beaches were all pre-sighted by the Germans from every artillery emplacement, Tobruk emplacement, and machine gun emplacement.

Resistance increased substantially as the landing craft approached the beaches. Smaller German weapons focused on the smaller wooden landing craft, while larger guns and artillery targeted the larger LCTs. Craft were taking hits all over the place, but they kept going. The landing craft were manoeuvring erratically, trying to dodge artillery, mines, and obstacles while fighting a nasty cross-current. The first landing craft approached the shoreline and the ramps dropped. The invasion had begun.

Andrew Irwin, Royal Canadian Navy

There was one instance where there was a German rail gun — you know, ran up and down the shore on rail tracks and of course they'd take a couple of shots at you and then they'd run up the track. You'd fire where they used to be and then the next thing they'd be firing from another position — so it took us quite a while to get rid of that one.

August Herchenratter, Highland Light Infantry

The gun emplacements — they were huge. All the way along the coast they had the big guns to help them and they were on solid cement and under them there was just a dugout, and that's where they were living. They were way up on the hill as you went in, and they fired down from there.

Doug Barrie, Highland Light Infantry

The initial landings were varied per beach. From offshore, watching the bombardment going on and the seventh and eighth brigades doing their landings, we could smell and see what was going on. The smoke and the shells — and there were shells coming out towards us too and plopping around in the sea. But I didn't see any hit any of our boats there, and I think they were concentrating mainly on the ones that were at the landing. I don't recall any German aircraft coming over, so it was quiet that way. The battleships that were out further were firing inland, and the shelling that was going on overhead was tremendous. The planes that had finished their bombing were along there and there were a few fighters coming around and strafing.

Naval personnel aboard HMCS *Prince Henry* at their station behind a No.9 Oerlikon gun.

View facing west of Nan Green beach, 2003.

Charles Fosseneuve, 13th Field Artillery

We fired two hundred rounds per gun over the Saskatchewan infantry [Royal Regina Rifles] to protect them, so the Germans would go and hide. They were going in there, the whole regiment like that, and we fired over their heads — we didn't lose many men in there.

View of Juno Beach at Courseulles-sur-Mer on D-Day.

Jack Read, Royal Regina Rifles

The captain who was directing my ship to land was pretty astute in that he seemed to be able to miss all these obstacles. We got in and eventually the doors on the landing craft came down, which was the signal for us to proceed. That we did. Fortunately we were in far enough that we didn't sink. We were in just three or four or five feet of water and our Bren gun carriers were capable of proceeding through that and up onto the beach.

At 0745, tanks of the 1st Hussars hit the beach facing Courseulles-sur-Mer and immediately engaged the German positions there. Courseulles-sur-Mer had a harbour and was the most heavily defended stretch of the Atlantic Wall in that area. The Germans had dug in and placed two 75mm, one 88mm, and four Tobruk positions, as well as six concrete machine gun posts. The tanks of the 1st Hussars quickly neutralized the emplacements while the Royal Regina Rifles landed and secured the German strongpoints. Some Royal Regina Rifles troops were lost when a landing craft hit a mine near the beach. The 13th Field Artillery provided supporting fire during this landing.

Philip John Cockburn, 1st Hussars

I landed with the 1st Hussars tank corps, 6th Armoured Regiment. In those days Courseulles was pretty small, and we were on the right flank. I can remember getting out of the tank — we were the only tank there. The infantry was all on the beach there, the few that there were. There was this officer, he had his eye hurt with a sniper bullet, and just about that time they were shooting at us. All of this happened within three minutes, maybe less. It was just rifle fire and machine gun fire, and they were pinging off the tanks, so we looked at one another and

Above: Canadian tanks land at Courseulles-sur-Mer. Many tanks were lost due to heavy seas on the way into shore.

Top Left: A Canadian Sherman tank in downtown Courseulles-sur-Mer serves as a monument to the Canadian forces that liberated the town on D-Day. (2003)

Bottom Left: Plaque from the Sherman tank monument in Courseulles-sur-Mer. (2003)

thought, "This is not a good place to be." When we were training, whenever we got landed we'd deflate the thing and all have a smoke and a chit-chat and come in and carry on. But it was more real than we were ever trained for. There wasn't a lot of fire, just machine gun fire. Our next step was to take out the emplacements. There was a church steeple just beyond at about ten o'clock and a good city block or more away from the water, and that's where we figured the sniper was. I was the gunner that day.

Philip John Cockburn, 1st Hussars

Everything was sort of bunged up. Nobody knew which way we were going in because we lost 80 percent of our tanks. We got in a whole lot more trouble because we lost a whole lot of guys. All kinds of them. If the navy had just put us on the beach, then that wouldn't have happened and that would have went smooth. For some reason they dumped us.

Left: A German artillery gun still stands in place by the mouth of the Seulles River in Courseulles-sur-Mer. (2003)

Right: Canadian Churchill tank. A monument just off Mike Sector beaches. (2003)

Left: Courseulles-sur-Mer was heavily fortified due to its port. (2003)

Right: A monument in the centre of Courseulles-sur-Mer commemorates the liberation of the town by Canadian forces on D-Day. (2003)

A monument to the Royal Regina Rifles stands beside the entrance to the beach at Courseulles-sur-Mer. (2003)

Jack Read, Royal Regina Rifles

As far as my particular group, we didn't actually hit anything for the first half-hour or so, but at that time, particularly on our left flank, there were skirmishes with our troops. Not of my group, but of our regiment. We could see where they were fighting at the edge of the rise. They landed at a little bit of a knoll. Our first problem in my group was getting over the barbed wire and over the sand dunes. The tanks were able to negotiate a route in the sand so that other vehicles like ours could proceed.

Minutes after the landing by the 1st Hussars and the Royal Regina Rifles, the Royal Winnipeg Rifles landed west of Courseulles-sur-Mer, on the other side of the Seulles River. Their landing craft came under heavy fire as they approached the shoreline. One LCA heading for Mike Sector in the area of Graye-sur-Mer was hit by a shell, and twenty men were killed before even making it to shore. In contrast to the Royal Regina Rifles, the Royal Winnipeg Rifles arrived before the tanks and faced withering fire with no cover and only small arms to attack with. The results were horrific. Many died before making it to shore. Others drowned. The company landing at Mike Red was decimated, and those who survived advanced to the sand dunes and tried to muster unit strength and organize their attack. In short, it was a bloodbath.

Jim Parks, Royal Winnipeg Rifles

When we were approaching the beach we could see it was just the way it was on the maps. We knew there were these pillboxes — there were five of them — and we even picked out the spot where we were going to set up our mortars on the beach. Coming in, it was the second

Mike Red beach at low tide. The men of the Royal Winnipeg Rifles had a long run in without any cover whatsoever. The result was catastrophic. (2003)

pillbox on the right of the river Seulles in Courseulles-sur-Mer. There was one big pillbox on the corner, the next one in is where we were going to be setting up our mortars near. On the pictures you could see a little bit of an indentation of the sand that had gone a little bit further in.

During planning they had a large sand table with all the names in the pictures and all the names on the sand table. They used fictitious names because they didn't give out to where we were landing. We knew it was going to be France, we didn't know *where* in France. They described to us what would happen prior to us going

Left: Mike Red beach at low tide, facing west towards Mike Green beach. (2003)

Right: Mike Red beach at low tide. (2003)

in. The three church spires we could see which were the three beaches that the Canadians were landing at — they would be bombed out by the air force. There was only one pillbox they really knocked out, because it was hit from the side — that was the one by Graye-sur-Mer. We had a good idea of what we were up against but they kept saying, well it's second-rate troops, it's people who had ulcers and something wrong with them — flat feet — but you put anybody regardless of what condition they're in behind a trigger, they can pull it. It's the same bullet fired by an SS or a guy with stomach ulcers.

As it turned out, things weren't knocked out. Things were actually still there. The pillboxes were still firing. I guess we were getting close to H-Hour and we were to land about two minutes prior. Well, they were opening up: the big LCTs were loaded with about three thousand rockets each. I guess they reloaded them but they had that many rockets and they would land as a blanket of explosions on the target they'd pick. If you ever hear those going ... it's scary.

It was a lot of noise and as we got closer — the water's still rough, mind you — we could see a couple of tanks in the water that were floundering. They were supposed to have gone in earlier. I remember seeing this tank that was sinking — it had this helium apparatus around it to keep it floating — that's a Sherman tank, but the men were climbing out of it because it was leaking and they were trying to get everybody out. I remember two or three guys were still on the turret and a couple of them got away, swam out and got away — but they were being fired upon too because at that time there was machine gun fire coming from the beach. We could see some spouts coming in from hitting the water. As we got closer the front end of our landing craft was hit by a shell that came through where the sailor was in the compartment to lower the ramp of the LCT. He came out all bloodied, and people said, "Get down," because we could hear all this *crack-crack-crack* of the small arms fire going over our heads and then the *ping-ping-ping* on the side of the landing craft. Another one came through and it hit the bulldozer blade near the top and sort of kissed off — and he said, "What the hell was that?" It was an armour-piercing shell that hit the top of the blade of the bulldozer and that's pretty thick — took a gouge out of it. So we were pretty safe 'cause we were in between the walls of the LCTs and we also had the Bren gun carriers, which had a quarter-inch of armour. We were pretty safe there. To my right I don't remember seeing much — I was focused on what the hell was happening in front of me.

Francis Godon, Royal Winnipeg Rifles

Coming in on the landing craft was something — the tide was ahead of us. The landing craft circled and dropped the ramp and you had to get off. When I jumped out you had water up to here and you had to hold your rifle up so you wouldn't get it wet — well, my rifle was no good anyway when I hit the beach.

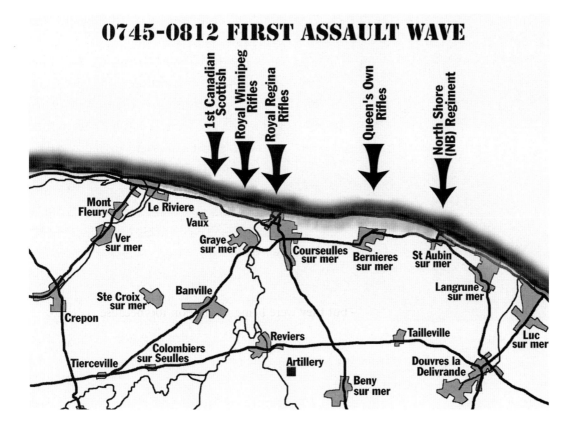

0745-0812 FIRST ASSAULT WAVE

1st Canadian Scottish · Royal Winnipeg Rifles · Royal Regina Rifles · Queen's Own Rifles · North Shore (NB) Regiment

Mont Fleury · Le Riviere · Vaux · Ver sur mer · Graye sur mer · Courseulles sur mer · Bernieres sur mer · St Aubin sur mer · Ste Croix sur mer · Banville · Langrune sur mer · Crepon · Reviers · Tailleville · Luc sur mer · Colombiers sur Seulles · Artillery · Douvres la Delivrande · Tierceville · Beny sur mer

Above: View from Courseulles-sur-Mer across the Seulles River of Mike Red beach, the landing site of the Royal Winnipeg Rifles. (2003)

Centre: The remains of a German concrete emplacement on Mike Red beach. In time, most of the fortifications on the beach have sunk into the sand. (2003)

Bottom: Detail of damage done by the artillery barrage to a German concrete emplacement. The combination of reinforcing metal rods and concrete that was several feet thick made them practically impregnable. (2003)

Jim Parks, Royal Winnipeg Rifles

Then we got in close enough that they dropped off the armoured bulldozer, which had long ropes with grappling hooks. The whole purpose of the ropes and hooks was to hook onto the barriers [hedgehogs, etc.] that were in the water, pull them ashore so that the landing craft could follow in. But as the bulldozer pulled off the landing craft and they told us to unload — the first carrier went off with the mortars in it, and he just went in and submerged. In the water, sunk, and the guys floated away and they were grabbing on to compo boxes and other things too — one of them grabbed onto one of the ropes of the armoured bulldozer.

And then the hollering of the commander of the boat: "Everybody get off the boat, start getting off." When that carrier went in, it just went. It was built to go four feet, and it just sank right in and it pulled the trailer off with it. The next one in was ours — the same bloody thing. We just went in the water and sank right down. I was sinking, Bob — this other crew member — he says, "Geez, unbuckle." We didn't have much on anyway because we had to be all set to grab the mortar plate and bombs and carry them in. Our rifle would stay in the carrier anyway. It was up to our shoulders and you'd give a little shove with your feet — I had my feet on the side of the reinforcing waterproofing and that's when I gave myself a shove off.

I was trying to keep down because you could hear this crackle. That's when they're coming over your head — there's a snapping sound. You know to keep your head down or it's going to snap into you. The one that you don't hear is the one that gets you. I remember seeing those guys dead in the water. We just headed out — I was pushed to one side because the waves were sort of coming and the wind was pushing you right to left. I must have got right in the path of the LCA coming in, because one of them sort of brushed my shoulder and I went underwater and I said screw it. When you're going up and down in the water as the waves come, my foot touched bottom when I was underwater and that sort of gave me a little bit of incentive to get up higher. So I popped up and there was one of the obstacles sitting there — these barriers — so I grabbed that. It had an old wine bottle filled with explosives and it had the fuse on the top. We were running towards the beach and I grabbed a couple of men struggling in the water and Bob Hussey he grabbed a couple and we just pulled them in.

Francis Godon, Royal Winnipeg Rifles

Aerial reconnaissance photo of Courseulles-sur-Mer, the Seulles River, and Mike Red beach during the landings.

After we hit the beach the real trouble started. You couldn't stand still, it didn't matter if this guy was yelling, you had to go because once you've stopped, you've had the bird. When they open the ramp, well, that means go. Don't stand because if you stand right there the machine guns are going to be after you and you couldn't wait for anybody, you had to go. If you stayed still — you were a target. So long as you were moving — they were guessing. You had to keep them guessing, let's put it that way, when you're on the beach you had to keep them guessing.

Crawl here, then run here, then crawl here — you couldn't come up in the same spot.

Left: Mike Red beach, facing west. (2003)

Right: The concrete German emplacement positioned nearest to the mouth of the Seulles River on Mike Red beach. (2003)

Tanks of the 1st Hussars and troops of the Royal Winnipeg Rifles and the Royal Regina Rifles landing near Courseulles-sur-Mer.

Jim Parks, Royal Winnipeg Rifles

You're just concerned with where you're at. You're looking right ahead of you. We later found out that was the greatest concentration of pillboxes faced by anyone in the Allied landing force.

Ron Gunson got wounded coming off and he tried to hide and they kept sniping at him. They kept picking away at him and wounded him a second time. That must have been pretty rough on him because his brother was on the same boat and he was killed right on the beach. You waited so long to die so fast. You think about it, all your people trained for all that time, and a lot of them had gone just that short time. You look around and where's all your buddies, all the people you know?

They were shelling and one of the smoke bombs apparently fell short and one man was covered with phosphorous, and you know what phosphorous is like — it burns on air? Him and his pal, they managed to get all his burnt clothes off.

Some of the other crew members were more to our right and they were doing some of the same things as I was doing. Bales and Holmes, they couldn't swim very well. They managed to make their way to the furthest lines of these barriers from shore and every time the waves came over they were being submerged, but they were hanging on for dear life. As we got in, I ran towards this one chap and

Top Left: Detail of the door side of the German emplacement nearest to the mouth of the Seulles River on Mike Red beach. (2003)

Bottom Left: Concrete base of a German emplacement overlooking Mike Sector. (2003)

Right: Monument to the Allied forces who liberated France, situated at the beach in Mike Sector. (2003)

I lay down. It was Corporal Scaife, but it turned out he was dead. Since I had no weapon I just grabbed his Sten gun and I grabbed his small pack. I had what they called an ablution kit for shaving and all that. I had that stuff and it was his.

I made my way to the pillbox on the right. We got there and we turned around and saw the Holmes and Bales were still stuck out in the water. So I went to the bulldozer and I said, "Geez, is there any way you can get these guys off?" So the guy took the bulldozer towards where they were. He got as far as he could and Holmes and Bales made their way to the blade and hung on and he backed up. While this was happening the small arms fire had quieted down but there was still mortar fire.

An impressive monument to the Royal Winnipeg Rifles located by the beach in Courseulles-sur-Mer. (2003)

Left: German emplacement located on Mike Red beach, one of the causes of great bloodshed on D-Day. (2003)

Right: Reminiscent of the parable of the man who built his house on sand, the German emplacements have suffered over the years. Like the Reich that was to last one thousand years, they were not to be. (2003)

Bob and I got Corporal Martin. He was moaning and we got him up to the pillbox and got him under cover. Meanwhile there were a lot of people coming in. First thing you know it was our next group coming in and my brother was one of them. Corporal Martin said, "Hold me, I'm cold," and so I was holding him for a while. He was badly racked with machine fire right across the midriff. His lungs were going — there were bubbles of blood from his mouth — and he passed away in a matter of about a minute. I found out later he had a young kid that he never saw, a young boy he had in England.

Francis Godon, Royal Winnipeg Rifles

My rifle didn't work because of the water, so I had to use my grenades and then I picked up a rifle from a dead German and used his rifle 'til I got a new one.

That was the biggest problem — how can you fight with no rifle and all these machine guns and these pillboxes? We had to use our grenades. We couldn't get in the pillboxes. If we had two guys, one would jump on the other and then jump on top of the pillbox and then he'd get in there and try and throw the grenade and make sure it fell inside — that's how we had to get the guns out.

By 0800 hours, Canadian forces had secured their first beachhead at Courseulles-sur-Mer in Mike Sector. The Royal Regina Rifles, covered by the tanks of the 1st Hussars, seized most of the German strongpoints and proceeded to battle the Germans in intense street-by-street, house-by-house fighting. One lone concrete emplacement with a 75mm gun held out on the shoreline, but it would be overcome by 0945.

Arthur John Allin, 14th Field Regiment

The first wave was infantry with artillery right close behind them. We gave covering support when the infantry went in. We were just going in and everybody had their heads down. I was a little bit snoopy and I stuck my head up and I could see what the hell was going on. Everything seemed to be going up and the rest of it was coming down. It was quite a turmoil. I tapped on the head of one of the chaps down in the gun crew and I said, "Come on up here and see what's going on." So he stood up and he says, "Holy mackerel! If this keeps up, somebody's going to get hurt." At that I started to laugh, because people *were* going to get hurt. Whether he had a strange sense of humour, I'm not quite sure, but I enjoyed it very much anyhow.

As we approached the shore, we were firing continuously. That was on the landing craft tanks. We fired until we reached very close to shore. We just kept up a

Left: The crew of HMCS *Prince David* help bring aboard Lieutenant Jack Beveridge, who was wounded by an exploding mine.

Right: A dead German on Juno Beach. A famous image, as it was one of the first pictures of the invasion of France.

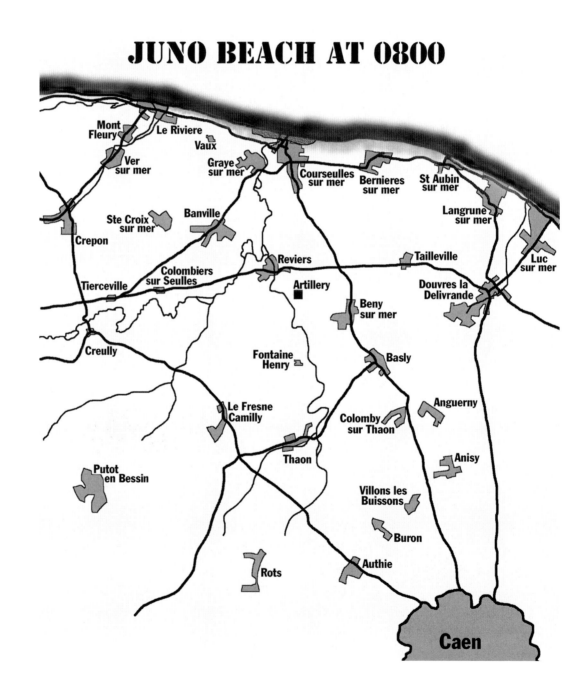

JUNO BEACH AT 0800

steady barrage until we got right near the land, and we had to turn around and go out a couple of thousand feet and turn around and come back. The reason for that was that we had to be able to fire the shells where it would do the most good to help the infantry. When we finished firing the shells, we had to throw all of the rest of the ammunition overboard, which just looked like a hell of a waste of ammunition. Then you soon realized that the self-propelled guns couldn't manoeuvre so they could back up, and go sideways, and everything else, to get out of the landing craft. They were just packed right in, side by side, and they just couldn't make it. So we had to do that to be able to give a little bit of manoeuvrability and to be able to leave the landing craft.

Jack Read, Royal Regina Rifles

There were a lot of buildings around that the Germans could hide behind. That part is difficult in any kind of fighting, whether it's street fighting or house-to-house. It's pretty tough going. The Germans were particularly good at it, especially at that particular point. It was damn annoying and scary. We were having difficulty getting through. They were in front of us and they were on the right of us and on the left of us

Monument to the 1st Canadian Scottish at the entrance to the beach at Courseulles-sur-Mer. (2003)

and we just had to keep going. Normally what you do is send in a couple of men to a particular position, and they would take up that position and hold it there. And then the next group of us would attack to that position and so you leapfrog as much as you can. Position to position, to doorways and outbuildings and whatever would be giving them some cover. A lot of the people who had been in the attack and were wounded were making their way back, or trying to make their way back, to protection and cover.

Watching the invasion from the flag deck of HMCS *Prince David*.

Andrew Irwin, Royal Canadian Navy

Once we started firing all we could hear was our own stuff going. You could see what was happening as the troops hit the beach, and then the close fire started up. We were in about fifteen hundred yards offshore — we could see a fair amount. We had the landing craft going by us, and you could see them hitting the beach and the ramps going down.

From their vantage point overhead, the bombers, fighters, and reconnaissance aircraft of the RCAF had the best view of the battle raging below.

Richard Rohmer, RCAF

When we got to the beachhead it was a wall of cloud that we had to get under. Taylor and I went up and down the Canadian and British beaches at five hundred feet — just as the first landing craft were coming in. We watched them come in and we could see out at the horizon — there was black smoke along the horizon from the battleships out there firing. We could see winking lights — little tiny winking lights and they were the battleships firing. So it was a fascinating sight, the most interesting sight I've ever seen.

We saw some men get out and charge up the beach. There were enormous explosions, of course. In fact, we were flying through these shells and really didn't understand that we were doing that — we couldn't see them. It was clearly a very dangerous situation. There was some flak coming at us from the German anti-aircraft, so we were getting our fair share of getting shot at.

I was absolutely, totally mesmerized — engrossed by the sight. It had never happened before, and it hasn't happened again. It was a brand new experience, it was highly dangerous, it was exhilarating. For me, I always say I had the best seat in the house, because I could see all this, and it's embedded in my mind. I can see it all whenever I want to conjure it up, which is one of the great things of the human mind. It was a fantastic sight.

Cec Brown, RCAF

When we got over there to patrol, we'd look down and see the guys coming out of these landing craft. The door would go down and they'd come out into water with their rifles up to keep them dry. We had a grandstand seat. We were flying at fifteen hundred feet — we were at the lowest level of fighters. We had fighters stacked up to fifteen thousand feet. You could almost recognize the people out there. The Germans [Luftwaffe] never showed up that day. They were very wise and they stayed away — they were so badly outnumbered. We never had to fire our guns.

Cec Brown, a Spitfire pilot who patrolled the skies over Juno Beach on D-Day. (2003)

We had a first-class seat to watch everything going on. Unfortunately I saw a friend get killed — he was with 421 Squadron. Johnny Drope is his name, and he got plastered from flak from the ground. He called his CO and said, "I'm having trouble, the engine's quitting, what should I do?" The CO says, "Well, you better bail out, there's no place for you to land down there in that water, it's crowded." I just happened to be looking in his direction. I saw him climb over the side and jump, and his parachute never opened. Johnny went all the way down and hit the Channel.

It was just unimaginable the organization that they put together for that, because everything had to be right on time. It's something that's hard to comprehend. It was overpowering. It was just so immense. The thought went through my mind: "How in the hell did they ever plan this to come out at the same time — all these ships, planes?" The planning behind it was just amazing. It was just breathtaking to see it all happen and to realize that the planning behind it was meticulous — they just hadn't forgotten a thing.

Paratroops were still being dropped — we could see them going in and dropping in.

Turned out later I had some friends over there and I didn't know they were there. I learned later too that my cousin, who was just a month or so older than I was, was there too in the army and landing and I didn't know where he was. Everything moved pretty quickly. The beach was crowded with people. Another wing would be coming in to relieve us and we had radio of course and said, "Sample One we're ready to come," and Sample One would be our leader and we'd get the hell out of the way and the other wing would take over. Boy what a job. Glad I wasn't down on the beaches.

While the men of the RCAF had a tremendous view of things, they also had a job to do — and they had to be aware of the dangers they were facing themselves.

Richard Rohmer, RCAF

When I was over the beaches at five hundred feet watching the first landing craft come in, I looked at my petrol gauge and it said zero. I had been so transfixed by what I was seeing I hadn't watched my gauge. When you're flying number two to somebody in a fighter, you use up more petrol than your leader does. I was quite alarmed by the fact that the gas gauge said zero. We immediately climbed back up to fifteen hundred feet and headed for England. I pulled my throttle back as far as I could to stay airborne and I leaned the engine out so that I used a minimum amount of gas on the way back. At that point if I had had to bail out I was quite prepared to do so. I felt very confident that if I had to jump out I would get picked up by one of those hundreds of ships on the surface. In a Mustang you don't ditch — that is, you don't put the aircraft onto the water because it has a big scoop under it and if you try to ditch it — land it in the water — the scoop catches the water and the aircraft goes straight in like a shark. You can go right to the bottom, and that's the end of the matter. So you have to jump out.

I landed at a place called Thorney Island, which is a Royal Air Force station on the south coast. I went straight for it and as I touched down my engine quit, that's how close it was. My number one went on to our base at Odiham. Once I was out of my aircraft I looked into the gas tank and I could see the bottom very clearly — there was nothing there. The local RAF contingent refuelled my aircraft and I took off for my Royal Air Force base just to the west of London, about forty miles north of Thorney Island. It was an exciting day.

At Courseulles-sur-Mer, the initial landing companies were soon joined by the Royal Regina Rifles' C and D Companies in a follow-up landing. D Company suffered massive losses on the beach due to mines, and only forty-nine survived to join the engagement in the town.

The bitter combat in Courseulles-sur-Mer had been anticipated, and the Royal Regina Rifles had received specialized training for street fighting beforehand. The town was broken up into twelve zones, and the companies were each assigned a specific area to clear. The going was slow and very dangerous, and the narrow roads and houses made it a sniper's paradise. The battle for Courseulles-sur-Mer would continue until the late afternoon.

Further west in Mike Sector the Royal Winnipeg Rifles saw two very different types of action on the beach. Just on the other side of the Seulles River the Royal Winnipeg Rifles had suffered carnage under the ferocious fire of the German emplacements. Massive numbers of casualties covered the beaches, and bodies were washing in with the incoming tide. But even further west, other companies landed to find that the German emplacement had been taken out by the naval barrage, and the only resistance that they had to overcome was small arms fire. The Royal Winnipeg Rifles neutralized those defences and secured the beach, then began to move inland. They battled machine gun posts and Tobruk positions and overcame them. They then moved inland to Graye-sur-Mer, a small village just west of Courseulles-sur-Mer and south of the beaches.

The wounded await evacuation at the seawall.

Jim Parks, Royal Winnipeg Rifles
We went and tried to pull more guys out of the water. Some were gone. Some that we pulled out earlier, they sort of got more water around them. Some of them might have been dead, and some would have been alive, I can't recall. A lot of them that were shot were shot across the stomach because the Germans set the machine

gun fire so that it's two and four feet above the level, so it'd just rake the beach and catch you right between the knees and the chest. So that's where most of the wounds were on people I'd seen.

All around me you could see the people on the barbed wires. They threw themselves on the barbed wire so that they could get through. We were trained to do that — fall on the wire and squash it down so that somebody could step on your back and jump over further. So instinctively we just grabbed people that were still floating in the water and pulled them as far as we could and dropped them. The whole area we had roughly 130 casualties along the beach. There were a few that were wounded on the beach that carried on and went through and they sent them back later on in the day. I don't know if they're counted or not. They were walking wounded.

Jack MacLean was one of those. He didn't know how badly he was hit in the back of the hip, until it stiffened up on him and somebody took a good look and said, "Jack you'd better get back." He was able to walk but he ended up in the hospital for a few weeks before he got back. We had roughly 130 or so and tack on what we had a couple of days later and we ended up with a total of about 450 people in a matter of two days that we lost. A few we had missing in action — we have about thirteen still listed as missing, presumed dead.

Near Courseulles-sur-Mer the men of the Royal Winnipeg Rifles and the Royal Regina Rifles, with the tanks of the 1st Hussars, fill the beaches.

Arthur Perry, 7th Canadian Infantry Brigade

We were right behind the Winnipeg Rifles actually. They were the first wave to go in, I guess — the Winnipegs, the Canadian Scottish, and the Regina Rifles. It was a little rough weather-wise. We landed all right but we hit a mine. We had to wait to get the ramp down flat enough so we could get our vehicles off. So we had to wait probably ten minutes I guess — it seemed like forever — before we could get off. There was only one pillbox where we landed and we saw this white flag come up like they were surrendering. I don't know whether they caused a little bit of trouble for the Winnipeg Rifles when they went in first, but they took quite a beating. Once we got the ramp down and got our vehicles off we were gone to our assembly area. All our boys got off in one piece anyway, and you thank the Lord for that.

Jim Parks, Royal Winnipeg Rifles

The brigade headquarters came in and there was a sergeant major. They needed a runner [messenger], so I was designated as a runner for about half a day. During that I got sick from the seawater and I ended burping it all up. Apparently I swallowed quite a bit. It could have been a culmination of that and all that excitement and gory things that you saw. Because you know most of the people that you saw. You might not have known their names — seven hundred or eight hundred people, you don't know all their names — but you know them to see them. Some had characteristics that you'd associate with them, you recognize them. Scaife we knew him because he was pretty good on the tug of war team, and Bull Klos, a chap that got mortally wounded but he went in and they found him in the pillbox with his hands around a German soldier's neck. He died that way and so did the soldier.

There were a lot of things that we heard later, but you can't see everything. I just know these people that we dragged in. The sergeant major used to be an old neighbourhood cop of mine. He used to come around the neighbourhood when we were kids and he knew me, and he said, "You just lie down there Parksie by that tree for a while and when you feel better you come on over."

Further west, still in Mike Sector, the Canadian Scottish landed. They immediately captured a German emplacement and then proceeded inland towards Graye-sur-Mer, where they would hook up with the Royal Winnipeg Rifles. While there was some action on this stretch of Juno Beach, it was not nearly as intense as in other places, and the Canadian Scottish suffered the fewest casualties of any Canadian assault battalion on D-Day.

At 0810 hours, the North Shore Regiment landed in Nan Sector at St. Aubin-sur-Mer. They immediately came under intense fire. This stretch of Juno Beach was particularly nasty due to a very high seawall that was lined with German fortifications and gun positions (including a 50mm gun in a concrete bunker), none of which had been knocked out by the naval bombardment. The North Shore Regiment found itself in a virtual shooting gallery. As the tanks of the Fort Garry Horse arrived, they were immediately destroyed by the 50mm gun mounted at the top of the seawall.

The solution was to move along the wall away from the German strongpoint, climb up, and then move through St. Aubin-sur-Mer to outflank the concrete bunker. This advancement was a tough battle, and it took the better part of the morning to accomplish. In the end, the emplacement was silenced. To the west, A Company of the North Shore Regiment arrived on the beach with tanks of the Fort Garry Horse, facing very little opposition.

Frank Ryan, North Shore (NB) Regiment

We landed right on the edge of the town. There was a seawall there that the village runs right along. If you looked up from the beach you would see sandbars and what-not, so no one could land there and there was a gap between us and the Third British Division — I think about four or five miles.

I was the assault section leader on D-Day. I was a corporal at the time. My job was to get on the beach first and to blow the barbed wire. We carried a lot of ten-foot lengths of bangalore torpedo, which is steel pipe. We had an aluminum ladder and equipment for crossing over barbed wire. I'm right in the front, I'm the first one off, and there's a ramp there at an angle and I could stand up and see. There wasn't any shelling or anything going on then; we were quite a little bit out in the water. Our assault craft was driven by a British corporal. Going in there was a shell that hit the water and a piece of the shrapnel hit his armoured plating, which has a peep site that he steers through. After the shell hit I saw him closing the peep site, and he went in blind.

Left: LCI (L) 135 en route to Juno Beach. An LCI could hold up to 388 soldiers.

Right: Landing craft of Force "J" off of the coast of France on D-Day.

German emplacement at St. Aubin-sur-Mer, now a monument of D-Day. (2003)

I was scared to death, there's no doubt about that. Anybody that says that they weren't scared, they're lying. I didn't enjoy it at all. You can die at any minute and there's mortar bombs and in some cases grenades thrown at you, and machine gun fire like you wouldn't believe. When we got in a little bit closer I looked up over the ramp and I could see the Germans' green tracer bullets.

Douglas Lavoie, Fort Garry Horse

Our squadron went in about five hundred yards and it was quite smooth then and we had no trouble getting to shore. Three of our tanks were sunk by enemy fire. B Squadron of our regiment never did put up their screens, their barges took them right in to the shore, so they had a dry landing.

Frank Ryan, North Shore (NB) Regiment

At St. Aubin you'd see that very high church steeple, and that was our landmark and I guess this English corporal who was driving the boat — that was his landmark too. And that's where we landed, just to the edge of the village. With the heavy seas the assault boat drifted to the left and he hit one of the girders there. Most of them had mines attached to them. He went in blind and he hit this damned steel girder in the water and he said, "Down ramp — abandon craft!" When he said that the two marines who had crawled along the side of the ship, on each side of the boat, they dropped the ramp and you had to go. When I looked, it was a hell of a long way from the beach.

Above: Motor launch escorting LCAs ashore from HMCS *Prince Henry*.

Left: Rare image of the first assault wave, the front of the landing craft just open to reveal the distant beach with obstacles and buildings in the background.

Right: Stepping out into intense crossfire, the Canadian infantry faced death with bravery, though many never made it more than a few steps ashore.

Canadian tank crews removing waterproofing from their tanks on the Normandy beachhead.

Douglas Lavoie, Fort Garry Horse

We landed at St.Aubin-sur-Mer. We were on the extreme left flank, and it wasn't as bad on the left as it was further on down the beach. A lot of the infantry took a pretty bad pounding — the Winnipeg Rifles and the Queen's Own and the Regina Rifles too. The Regina Rifles and the Winnipeg Rifles were supported by the 1st Hussars. The Queen's Own were supported by B Squadron of the Garrys. When we got on shore in our tank the screen wouldn't go down properly, so the crew commander said, "Okay Doug, you get out with your knives — you and Spence — and you're going to have to puncture all those tubes," which we did. We walked around the tank with our knives and punctured these tubes and we got back in the tank and we were okay. Some of the fellows said, oh yeah, there were a lot of shells, small fire, bouncing off of the tank, but Spence and I didn't notice that.

Landing on the beach at St. Aubin-sur-Mer.

Frank Ryan, North Shore (NB) Regiment

When I jumped there was a piece of shrapnel that hit me on the leg. Another fella and I were carrying equipment on a piece of wood. I ended up headfirst down in the English Channel. I still had a hold of that pole that we were carrying. So he pulled me up, and I said, "You hold that damned pole, I got to go down — I lost the Sten gun flailing in the water." Feeling around I found it, so I was a little late getting on the beach with my section. When we got on the beach there wasn't a piece of wire or anything on it. All of our explosives were gone. I had extra men in my section because of all the explosives and the ladder and three lengths of steel pipe and so on. But when I got on the beach I had only three men left and myself.

View of Nan Red beach, facing eastward to St. Aubin-sur-Mer and its sea-wall facing the ocean.

There wasn't a piece of wire on the beach whatsoever, not a thing, but there was a small seawall there, maybe ten to fifteen feet wide and about eight to ten feet high, and so the whole company piled up behind that. We were there quite a while and started getting picked off one at a time by a sniper over in A Company's area.

Below: Disabled landing craft from HMCS *Prince Henry* just offshore. A large percentage of Canadian landing craft were lost that morning due to artillery, mines, and obstacles.

Douglas Lavoie, Fort Garry Horse

We lost thirteen on D-Day. Now the North Shores that we were supporting lost about forty men. Killed — not just wounded. Forty men dead. They were shot by these snipers hiding in buildings, church steeples, just name it, but they were able to pick off forty of those young guys. We were on the beach by eight o'clock. We were supposed to be in earlier, but the best-laid plans of mice and men, they don't work like that. I'd say we were on the beach three-quarters of an hour to an hour. Once we got through, the whole day was

spent just going ahead as best we could. We really didn't have any heavy opposition. That might sound strange after hearing that forty infantrymen were killed, but as I said, most of those guys were picked off by snipers.

Left: Hunting for snipers at the front.

Right: Monument to the North Shore regiment at St. Aubin-sur-Mer.

Frank Ryan, North Shore (NB) Regiment

My lieutenant turned to call me, and when he did, the sniper shot him. I met him after the war and he told me that the bullet went in through his left arm, out past his heart, and out the back. He was on a very slow, small boat because there were a lot of casualties and he ended up in the hospital. They put him in a room to die three times — the black room I think he called it. But he didn't die. And in fact, he didn't die until

The high seawall presented serious problems for the men of the North Shore (NB) Regiment, and the German positions allowed the Canadians very little cover. (2003)

2001. He was behind the wall and I decided to just lay out in the front because with all of the company all piled up behind that little seawall, a couple of mortar bombs and you'd have a hell of a lot of casualties. Well, I thought I'd take a chance and lay on the beach, and then somebody called me and I ended up over there with the whole company.

Douglas Lavoie, Fort Garry Horse

The difference between our squadron and B Squadron was that B Squadron never got off the beach until sometime after lunch. The seawall was too much for them. We happened to have the English Churchills [tanks] there. They fired these huge fixed charges and blew a hole in the wall, then we drove through the hole. Major

Left: German emplacement at St. Aubin-sur-Mer. (2003)

Right: Interior of the German emplacement at St. Aubin-sur-Mer. (2003)

Brey, our commanding officer, led us through and we drove through the little town of St.Aubin-sur-Mer like nothing at all. When we got through there was a bunker that the Germans had taken refuge in, and they'd pop out once in a while and lob a grenade at the infantry, which was passing through. One of the North Shore officers asked us to clean up that bunker, which we did. Went in and fired a few rounds of 75mm and the German guys came out and surrendered. That was about it.

At 0812, the Queen's Own Rifles landed in Nan Sector at Bernières-sur-Mer. Their landing had been held up by the rough seas, but amazingly they arrived together. The German emplacements were hidden and positioned along the top of a seawall. When the ramps of the landing craft lowered, the men faced a horrible predicament. Immediately they were under fire. Many of the landing craft did not get all the way into shore due to sand bars and other obstacles, and so the men disembarked into deep water. Once they hit dry land, they had to race across 183 metres of beach without cover and under a heavy crossfire due to the fact that their tank support would be landing late. Anyone who stumbled or stopped was killed.

A hidden 88mm gun in a concrete emplacement decimated the lead platoon, eliminating two-thirds of the men, including all of the officers. Another company landed right in front of a German emplacement and lost half of its men in a very short span of time. The Queen's Own Rifles suffered sixty-five casualties in just the first few minutes of the invasion alone. So heavy was the fire across that stretch of Nan Sector that the few men who survived had defied the odds beyond comprehension. And they now faced a daunting task: to take out the fortified German positions with nothing more than small arms and hand grenades.

Joe Oggy, Queen's Own Rifles

When I stood up in the landing craft, the man in front of me had a pack on his back and I couldn't get down because of this. So the guys asked me what I could see. I was giving the boys a blow-by-blow description of what I was seeing there. That's B Company here, A Company there, C Company. Each landing craft had a platoon in there, so there were three platoons to a company. There were three of them coming in all at once, and what happened to the others I have no idea — I was only concerned with myself and my men. I was 2IC [second-in-command] — I wasn't the leading corporal, I was 2IC. You have a corporal in the front and a corporal in the back, and that was the way we were working it. I told them what was going on, so that kind of gave you more courage because they were under cover on both sides except the middle row. The shoreline was getting bigger and bigger, and I said, "Hey, we're just about there." Finally I heard this *whang!* coming over my head — *crack! crack-crack-crack* — and I tried to get down and I couldn't get down any further because of this guy's pack.

Left: German concrete emplacement at St. Aubin-sur-Mer. (2003)

Right: Landing craft heading for Bernières-sur-Mer from HMCS *Prince David* and SS *Monowai*.

View of Bernières-sur-Mer from the landing craft on approach.

Charles McNabb, Queen's Own Rifles

I know it was real early and I could actually see the beach. I was in the landing craft and when that ramp went down, they said there was only a couple of feet of water but I was up to my knees in it. The bunkers started firing at us and when we hit Bernières-sur-Mer, our aim was to hit the wall right away. But a lot of good men didn't go, and the beaches out there were red with blood, dying comrades. I'll always have that day in my mind. I'm short, and I was carrying a Bren gun, and I had to run and I must have did pretty good because no bullet got me. Although I did eighteen months in Korea, this was the worst experience I have ever had. I'll tell you, any man who says he wasn't scared, I'll show you a liar. My friend got to here and next thing he says is, "I'm hit." I never saw him again 'til last year [2002]. A lot of bad memories here … a lot of bad memories.

Rolph Jackson, Queen's Own Rifles

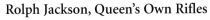

In my section of ten men, the sergeant was killed by this bloody pillbox. I was the eleventh man out of the landing craft in that group. Of the ten men in the section, seven were killed, two of us were wounded, and the only man that survived had never done a practice landing before. He landed with us as a reinforcement. He joined us thirty-one days before the sixth of June. The whole company was pretty badly decimated — we had over half the battalion's casualties. I don't know how

Top: German machine gun position after capture.

Centre: Convoy of LCIs during the first assault of the coast.

Bottom: Rockets fired from a landing craft were to soften the target before the landings began. At the very least, they created craters for cover on the beaches.

many actually were killed in the company — somewhere around thirty-four, thirty-five. When the platoon pulled off the beach, there were about nine people left. A lance-sergeant and six to eight riflemen, three of whom were wounded. Two of the wounded riflemen had been hit in the legs and couldn't walk very far — maybe a couple of miles — and they fell out.

View of Nan White beach, facing east, during the invasion.

Joe Oggy, Queen's Own Rifles

So when we got going in on D-Day I was in the middle row — there were three rows, and the middle row is the last one to get off and I was the last person. As these boys were jumping off the landing craft, the boat was drifting out all the time. So finally everybody was gone and I was all by myself in the middle and I thought, "I've got to get out of here." So I took a big run and jumped in the water and it was fairly deep — not over my head or anything but I ducked right down because I had some training out in British Columbia at the battle school there. We trained being in the water with just your head showing and from two or three hundred yards from the shore you couldn't even see the person because of the waves. So I did the same thing there and kept coming in more and more until finally I couldn't get down any lower with just my head. And looking at all the boys that were being killed because the Germans were up along this wall killing everybody that were coming in and I thought, well, we couldn't help anybody. We were warned — don't help anybody because then there's two gone instead of one. We need every man we can. So I just jumped up and charged and jumped over all the wounded and the dead and got right up against this wall.

Jack Martin, Queen's Own Rifles

Now the ship I was on was one of the few that made it right into shore and the ramp dropped right down onto the sandy beach. We normally had five men to a mortar carrier. A few minutes before we landed our sergeant said, "There's only two men allowed in with the carrier in case it hits a mine and blows up. So you three guys," and he pointed to me and Johnny Farrell the driver, and Ernie, "you'll go in with C Company as they are the reinforcements," which we did. When that ramp hit the sandy beach there was Major Charlie Dalton standing there with blood streaming down his face. He had been hit in the head, and he said, "Get up to the wall." Well I was at the wall before he finished his sentence. In those days we were really in good shape, and that month training in Scotland, you'd never see exercises like that. Landing from the craft, we had to cross the beach, jumping over equipment that was there and some bodies. You weren't allowed to stop and help anybody — there were shells exploding all over the place. But when I saw poor Charlie Dalton — he and his brother both commanded the assault companies A and B, and they were both very good friends of mine — when I saw poor Charlie with all that blood on his face … he knew he had to be evacuated but he stayed on the beach trying to help everybody all he could.

View from a German gun position at Bernières-sur-Mer on D-Day.

A group of landing craft heading for the beaches.

Roy Shaw, Queen's Own Rifles

I was wounded attempting to rescue one of my buddies along with another Queen's Own. Took about ten steps and I was wounded myself — a bad wound through the right shoulder. After I was hit, the sergeant major came over and got

German concrete emplacement on Nan White beach. This site is a monument to the men of the Queen's Own Rifles who stormed the beach at this location, and a memorial to all of those who lost their lives on this stretch of sand. (2003)

my gear off and dropped it in the ocean. We found out later he did the right thing because apparently my collarbone was left with a splinter and had that broken off, it would have punctured my lung, likely, and I probably would have drowned in my own blood. So by the grace of God I'm here.

By the next morning I was back in England at a casualty clearing station and then from the casualty clearing station I was moved to Horsham general hospital where I was operated on. All the other men that came after us deserve a great deal of credit because they went through far more than I did.

Joe Oggy, Queen's Own Rifles

The only thing I felt sorry for — we couldn't help anybody. We couldn't help anybody at all, because if you did, you were dead. Snipers were hiding in different places.

Rolph Jackson, Queen's Own Rifles

You remember bits and pieces. We had a lot of equipment that didn't get ashore. One of the lads was carrying a flamethrower, a portable. He landed in deep water and the flamethrower didn't work. Our landing craft got in fairly close; we were up to our waists in water, I always said below my crotch. I was hit in the water and knocked off my feet but most of the guys never got ashore. They were firing slightly across our front.

Nan White beach, facing west towards Courseulles-sur-Mer. (2003)

This pillbox is still there — it's a regimental memorial now. The half-timber house has got a sign on it. The Queen's Own liberated it; it was the first building in Normandy to be liberated because it was right on the beach.

Joe Oggy, Queen's Own Rifles

This watch … that's the one I had on D-Day. They told us we had fifteen minutes to live on the beach and I looked at my watch and scraped the sand and everything off it — twenty minutes and I'm still alive! So I kept it ever since. And my dog tags — when you're shot they cut one off and the other you leave with the dead body. My mother gave me a ring and it would always bother me because when you held your rifle, the ring would get caught in the parts of the rifle, so I had to take it off and I don't know what happened to it. I carried it on here but I lost the darn thing, and it had "from mother" inside of the thing, I was always sorry about that.

Rolph Jackson, Queen's Own Rifles

No Bren guns in our section in our boat got ashore. Anybody that was carrying anything but a rifle didn't make it. Seeing the guys go down in front of me. One of the lads — Ted Westerby — had a mickey in his pack and I saw Al Kennedy staggering. He had been hit — he was my Bren gunner, big guy — the gunner says, "Mickey." Al doesn't drink, this is what went through my mind, I'll remember this as long as I live, that Al didn't drink. He came to us from the Airborne — he washed out in Benning in 1943. One of the guys was grousing about having to carry the Bren. Al says, "Give me the goddamn thing, I'll take it," and he hung onto the Bren gun until he was killed.

Above: The first house liberated in France on D-Day, by the Queen's Own Rifles. One of the most famous buildings in Canadian history. (2003)

Left: Inscription of the plaque that stands outside of the house that the Queen's Own Rifles liberated.

We had two brothers in the platoon, great brothers. Doug was my number two on the Bren, Gord was in platoon headquarters. He had a Bren gun or a piat or a mortar — they were trained to handle anything extra, provide extra firepower if needed. They were both killed.

One of the lads who was killed got a "Dear John" letter about three weeks before we landed. Now that lady, if you can call her such, would get his widow's allowance. That's something that sticks in your craw.

At 0820 at Mike Sector, the few tanks of the 1st Hussars to get ashore were quickly destroyed. It was obvious that there were some sections of the beach that were still very hot.

By 0827 the beach at Bernières-sur-Mer had been secured, and the Queen's Own Rifles crossed the seawall and began to move inland. They faced minefields, machine gun fire, and mortars. Their advancement stalled for a short while due to the dogged defence of the Germans, but once the tanks of the Fort Garry Horse arrived, progress commenced once again. Before long the follow-up wave of the Queen's Own Rifles' reserve companies had arrived to reinforce the decimated units and ensure that the forward momentum would be maintained. This combination of events allowed the Queen's Own Rifles to advance through Bernières-sur-Mer quite rapidly, clearing the area of all Germans.

Rolph Jackson, Queen's Own Rifles

We didn't have much room and what people don't understand is how few people were there. On the initial landing 270 of the Queen's Own, 270 North Shore, 270 Regina Rifles, 270 Winnipeg Rifles — how many is that? A little over a thousand men. If there had have been major opposition they would have overrun us because we were spread thin.

To tell you how lucky I am, I shouldn't be here. I had the front of my uniform shot to tatters. I can tell you what bullets going through your clothes feels like. That was coming out of the landing craft, I was still in the water. If I had been half a step further ahead, I wouldn't be here. See I was hit in my hand and knocked off my feet and when I got up I had no section. I could see the bodies, see the blood, but no section.

Two of us out of the section crossed the wall ... Normandy was a meat grinder.

Joe Oggy, Queen's Own Rifles

Once I got up against the wall, it swooped up in the air and it would be about eight feet to the top. Well we got up to the wall — that was the main thing. There was reinforcing rods sticking up and one was bent over. I jumped up on there and got toggle ropes — a rope with a toggle that you hook together if we had to go up a cliff, you put them together to make one big one — and I took my toggle rope off, jumped up on this wall, and hooked it onto one of these rods. I thought,

Canadian troops crouch behind a concrete wall before going inland.

"I'll hook it on there and I'll get over the top of the wall." When I did I just heard *whoosh!* Bullets flying over my head and I fell right back down and I left my toggle rope up there — I didn't need it anymore. If it hadn't been for the hole in the wall we'd have had trouble.

Jack Martin, Queen's Own Rifles

I think the worst part was seeing our own guys lying on the beach dead or wounded. We got up to the wall and there was one of the riflemen from B Company — he had had one of his phosphorous grenades hit by a bullet. The phosphorous was burning him, so two men were dragging him down to the water to submerge him to put the fire out. One of our other fellas in B Company, his name was Stumpy Gordon, he had one of those flamethrowers, and the story is — I didn't see it — that when they hit the shore they were pinned down by a machine gun and he was going to be the big hero. So he gets up and he runs and zigzags right up to the bunker and puts the nozzle inside and pulls the trigger and all it was was a stream of liquid coming out — no ignition. The ignition had got wet. So he had to

A German pillbox near where the Canadians landed. A dead Canadian soldier lies on the slope.

just lay down and his buddy Rudy Lebuff threw a grenade in through the hole and silenced the gun. He was the pitcher for our baseball team. We waited and waited and crouched under the wall and then they told us to move along to our left and the engineers were just finishing putting up a ramp. Some of the vehicles — the tanks and that — made it up over the ramp, over the wall that way, but we used a hole that had been blown by one of our shells.

Joe Oggy, Queen's Own Rifles

So I just lay along that wall and somebody said that there was a hole in the wall. One of our ships fired a shell and right at the base put a hole right on the ground level, right through the wall. So when somebody hollered that there's a hole, I kept creeping up there and all the time the enemy were trying to get at me because I was still alive. So I got through the hole on the other side and when I did and stood up the ground was as tall as I was. The ground was so high that we were quite protected there. I took a sod and put it over my head and Stumpy Gordon came by and said, "What's wrong, Corp?" And I said, "I'm scared!" And he says,

The famous Queen's Own Rifles House in Bernières-sur-Mer on D-Day, and fifty-nine years later on June 6, 2003.

"So am I, come on!" And he gave me his water bottle because I took my pack off — I was afraid of getting caught in the hole. He gave me a drink and he says, "Give me my bloody water bottle back!" And he said, "C'mon let's go." Then I broke loose from there and felt a little better.

Rolph Jackson, Queen's Own Rifles

The wall was slowly being filled up now. Eight to ten feet above, and a concave away from you — most of our ladders were back in the water. Where we went over the wall further to the left, one of the landing craft had lost her rudder and drifted ashore and they got in pretty well complete because nobody was down there to stop them, the wall wasn't too high. We got through the wall. There was a hole — possibly four feet wide, five feet high. You could go through it just bending your head and we were through the wall. I don't know who took out the pillbox, but it was taken out. They sent me back to the beach for extra ammunition. Frank comes up to me and says, "Rolph, go down and see if you can pick up a couple of Brens and some Bren mags." So I did, I went back. It was a pretty sad looking beach. To see people you knew, knowing that they weren't ever going to fight again.

Joe Oggy, Queen's Own Rifles

So after that we just reorganized again. We did a pretty good job — some were shot up but we did all right there. Once we got through the hole in the wall, on the other side we ran across to a bunch of buildings. That's when I saw my first flail. A "flail" is a tank with a big drum on the front with chains, and when this drum goes around the chains beat the ground for mines. So we got in behind one of these and as it

Left: A flail tank was one of the strange devices that saved many Canadian lives on D-Day by clearing pathways through minefields.

Right: A flail tank in action. The drum would spin, flailing the chains around, setting off mines without any loss of life.

moved in beating the ground, it would pick up a mine and explode in the air. Part of the chain would go with it. We followed it all the way through. At the same time there were two white tapes being put out and as long as we stayed in those tapes we were fine. But when the tank stopped, an officer went around to talk to somebody in the tank and stepped on a mine. That's how foolish he was at that time — he was killed. I don't know who the officer was because we lost a lot of officers. They didn't know when to duck or something.

Jack Martin, Queen's Own Rifles

C Company was just coming ashore to my right so I and the other two fellas with me — Johnny Farrell and Osburn — we joined in with C Company. We went up and as we're going through the town, a sergeant from one of the rifle companies is marching right up in the middle of the road, and he's saying, "Keep into the wall, there's snipers all around," and I don't know how long he lasted because anyone walking right in the middle of the road would be an ideal target — especially with stripes on.

Left: Monument to the Queen's Own Rifles at Bernières-sur-Mer with Nan White beach in the background.

Right: Inscription on the plaque of the monument to the Queen's Own Rifles at Nan White beach.

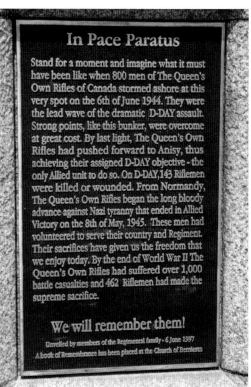

In Pace Paratus

Stand for a moment and imagine what it must have been like when 800 men of The Queen's Own Rifles of Canada stormed ashore at this very spot on the 6th of June 1944. They were the lead wave of the dramatic D-DAY assault. Strong points, like this bunker, were overcome at great cost. By last light, The Queen's Own Rifles had pushed forward to Anisy, thus achieving their assigned D-DAY objective - the only Allied unit to do so. On D-DAY, 143 Riflemen were killed or wounded. From Normandy, The Queen's Own Rifles began the long bloody advance against Nazi tyranny that ended in Allied Victory on the 8th of May, 1945. These men had volunteered to serve their country and Regiment. Their sacrifices have given us the freedom that we enjoy today. By the end of World War II The Queen's Own Rifles had suffered over 1,000 battle casualties and 462 Riflemen had made the supreme sacrifice.

We will remember them!

Unveiled by members of the Regimental family - 6 June 1997
A book of Remembrance has been placed at the Church of Bernières

Rolph Jackson, Queen's Own Rifles

We looked at things a little different than civilians — to this day we look at things a little different from the average civilian. I remember seeing the guys after crossing the wall, some of them from other platoons. In fact, a friend of mine came over to me and whacked me on the shoulder and said, "You made it Rolph!" Then he says, "You've been hit!" Because he had hit me on my right shoulder. I had taken a piece of shrapnel and didn't realize it. I had the skin nicked on my leg, too. I didn't feel it. Didn't know anything about it until I went to take my shoes off and the sock was full of dried blood.

Roy Shaw, Queen's Own Rifles

B Company, I think it was sixty-three we lost if I remember my counting, just from B Company alone. That's not counting the rest of the regiment. So we had a bad day that day. Many of them have said it was one of our worst days.

View of Nan White beach, facing west. (2003)

Rolph Jackson, Queen's Own Rifles

Once we got past the wall it was sporadic sniping. If there was fighting in Bernières, there was no major damage. Later on, yes, they ran into areas where there was opposition. We didn't take prisoners. I understood there were prisoners taken later, but we didn't take prisoners. We had nobody left to look after them. When you're down to nine men, you're not going to spend your time sending two men to guard prisoners.

Left: Tanks and supplies moving onto a busy beach on D-Day.

Right: Canadians on Juno Beach, with areas marked off.

Left: View facing east from Mike Red beach. (2003)

Right: Troops of Le Régiment de la Chaudière landing at Bernières-sur-Mer on D-Day.

Men of Le Régiment de la Chaudière arrive at Bernières-sur-Mer.

Left: View from LCI (L) 306 of naval group.

Right: LCI (L) 135 carrying men from the Highland Light Infantry and the North Nova Scotia Highlanders to Normandy.

At 0830 the remaining companies of the Canadian Scottish landed on the westernmost stretch of beach in Mike Sector. While there was some mortar fire, there was little resistance to the landing, and the unit was ready to move inland, though before doing so they faced a minefield that had to be cleared.

Meanwhile, the reserve battalions began to arrive at the beaches. Le Régiment de la Chaudière suffered losses when one of their landing craft hit a mine while coming ashore. Others drowned trying to make their way onto the beach. Once they finally arrived in Nan Sector at Bernières-sur-Mer, they found themselves under fire from a German emplacement that had not yet been silenced. They lined the seawall, getting out of the line of fire until the emplacement was cleared. The Chaudières then moved into Bernières-sur-Mer to follow the Queen's Own Rifles and do mop-up.

The rising tide presented a problem for the invading Canadian forces on the beach. The waters were obscuring the whereabouts of obstacles and mines. The width of the beach was getting smaller, making traffic denser and the congestion of men and materials worse as each minute wore on. The force of the current was pushing landing craft sideways into obstacles and mines. The results were deadly: of a total of 306 LCAs involved in the combat, 20 were lost in one battalion landing alone, and overall, 90 were lost or disabled during the course of the morning.

Also at 0830, the B Squadron 22nd Dragoons and the 26th Assault Squadron Royal Engineers arrived in Mike Sector with their flail tanks and their assault vehicles, Royal Engineers (AVREs). Flail tanks were a wonderful invention that would help clear a path through a minefield quickly and allow for the infantry to advance in safety. The beach was getting narrow in Mike Sector, and the anticipated exits from the beaches were not open — numerous exits from the landing beaches were to have been used for advancement inland. The first priority was to open Gap Number Two, which was a lane. The operation was dangerous, and several vehicles and pieces of equipment were lost to mines. But in the end, the exit was opened, and a flow of vehicles and supplies began to move inland. The Royal Engineers then set about opening the other exits from the beach.

A similar problem was faced in Nan Sector at Bernières-sur-Mer. The seawall had been constructed with a curved front edge that would not allow tanks to climb over it. The infantrymen were moving past the seawall through holes that had been created by the naval barrage. In an attempt to open an exit through the seawall, a tank and a bulldozer were lost. It was decided that they needed a ramp or a bridge over the seawall. Immediately they set about creating one, and once it was in place, several more were built.

Of all the hours on D-Day, this was the bloodiest. The successful landings on the beaches came at a huge cost. The bravery of the Canadians involved was outstanding, and a source of national pride. Many say that Canada became a nation at Vimy Ridge in World War I. Juno Beach is where Canada became a great nation.

JUNO BEACH AT 0900

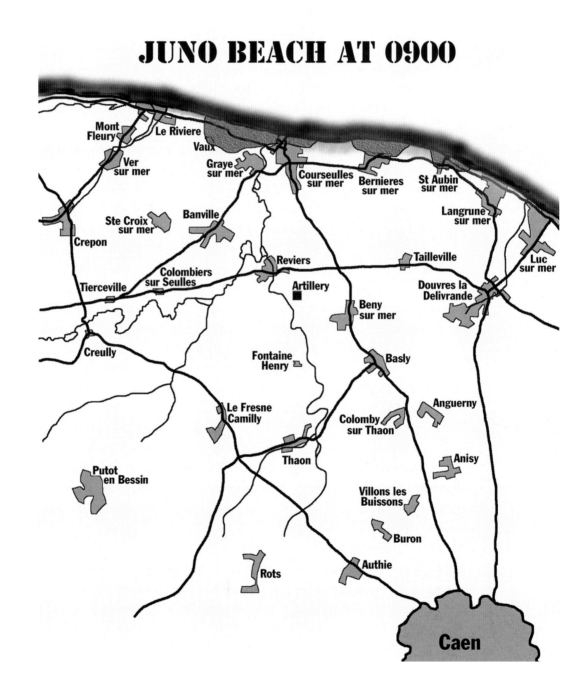

Mont Fleury
Le Riviere
Vaux
Ver sur mer
Graye sur mer
Courseulles sur mer
Bernieres sur mer
St Aubin sur mer
Langrune sur mer
Ste Croix sur mer
Banville
Crepon
Luc sur mer
Reviers
Tailleville
Colombiers sur Seulles
Tierceville
Artillery
Douvres la Delivrande
Beny sur mer
Creully
Fontaine Henry
Basly
Le Fresne Camilly
Anguerny
Colomby sur Thaon
Anisy
Thaon
Putot en Bessin
Villons les Buissons
Buron
Rots
Authie
Caen

By 0900 hours, all of the landing sites along Juno Beach had Canadian soldiers on them. Some sites were secure, but others were still being hotly contested. Despite the devastating losses early on, the Canadian troops were beginning to gain the upper hand, and the German defences beyond the fortifications along the shoreline were scattered and thin.

In Nan Sector, the North Shore Regiment continued to move through St. Aubin-sur-Mer in an effort to outflank the German emplacement at the top of the seawall that overlooked the landing site. The gun located there still posed a threat. The men of the North Shore Regiment fought along rue Marechal Foch and down rue Canet and rue Gambetta, moving in behind the large gun and its crew. Before long, the emplacement was completely surrounded.

Also in Nan Sector, closer to Courseulles-sur-Mer, two exits from the beach were cleared at 0900 hours. Tanks began to move inland and headed towards the town to aid the Royal Regina Rifles in clearing Courseulles-sur-Mer. The intense street fighting continued, and the tanks would give the Canadian troops the upper hand in the battle.

In Mike Sector the 1st Canadian Scottish had advanced inland, attacked the Vaux Castle (Graye sanitarium) with grenades, and captured it.

Charles Fosseneuve, 13th Field Artillery

Intense street fighting at St. Aubin-sur-Mer faced the North Shore Regiment as they tried to move inland.

I was a bombardier in artillery — a gun layer. We had about four feet of water when we landed and we had to drive in the water with our machines. We landed with the infantry almost. As soon as we finished firing these guns over their heads, we came behind and landed. There were people all over the area, but we saw a few people drown in the water. I don't think it was from machine gun fire — they just drowned, I think. Full equipment … I guess they were too heavy to swim. Lots of them died. A lot of them went through all right, but some were taken prisoner right away on the beach. When we landed the big German army wasn't there — we were lucky that

Landing on Juno Beach.

day. It was my birthday, June the sixth, when I came in. I never thought of my birthday that particular day; I was thinking ahead all the time, about the enemy.

At 0910 hours the 19th Field Regiment landed, bringing with them their self-propelled artillery for closer support for the advancing troops. Shortly thereafter the 13th Field Regiment landed at Courseulles-sur-Mer, right behind the Royal Regina Rifles. The Germans were stubborn in their defence of the town, and the Canadians were applying more and more firepower in order to dislodge them.

Further west in Mike Sector, Gap Number Two was being cleared. Flooding posed a problem, and a tank sank into the sand. But Canadian ingenuity prevailed, and the abandoned tank was used as a centre support for a bridge to make the gap passable for large vehicles. By 0915 hours, Gap Number Two was open and the flow of armoured vehicles inland commenced. Work began on Gap Number One, where minefields had to be cleared and enemy fire had to be silenced.

At 0925 the 14th Field Regiment finally landed, after having circled and fired a second round, then dumped ammo for the landing. They quickly unloaded their self-propelled guns and moved into position to support the advance inland. The beaches were beginning to fill up with men and equipment. The rising tide reduced the amount of space available along the beaches, and the congestion began to build. The Royal Engineers worked feverishly to open gaps in the seawall to allow for more troops to move inland sooner. Breaches in the seawall were exploited, and ramps were installed for vehicles and troops to drive and climb over.

Arthur John Allin, 14th Field Regiment

We landed at Bernières-sur-Mer, and our headquarters were at Courseulles. We landed at what has become a very famous landmark, a big house on the beach. When we landed we met with some very interesting fire from the enemy, and as we

approached there was a German 88 gun up some-where, and we couldn't see it, but it could see us. It knocked off three of our self-propelled guns out of a battery of eight. So we took a fair loss going in. They were carrying 105 gallons of high octane gas plus all the ammunition and when it went up it made one hell of a racket.

The interesting thing in going in was that just as we were landing, a sergeant from the beach party — which was a British organization that had landed and was directing us through the minefields — we just got in a few yards and this chap was smiling as if he was happy to do the job that he was doing, and he just stepped back off of the cleared area where the mines were being removed, and he stepped on a mine himself and he just blew up in a cloud of clothing and every-thing else. Right in front of my eyes. That was the first person I saw killed, so it was a little bit shocking.

It was surprising after we got inland just a little way to find out there were still pockets of Germans behind us that the infantry were mopping up. Some of the units went ahead to engage the enemy, to take out that 88 that had been bothering us, so we were happy to hear that.

Above Left: Wounded soldiers resting on the beach, awaiting transfer to the casualty clearing station.

Above Right: Canadian soldiers examining the German plans for the beach defences at Courseulles-sur-Mer.

By 0930 the Queen's Own Rifles and Le Régiment de la Chaudière had eliminated the snipers in Bernières-sur-Mer and secured the town. At the same time, over in Mike Sector, Gap Number One was opened up and the flow of men and material inland increased, overwhelming Graye-sur-Mer and heading towards Banville and Ste. Croix-sur-Mer. The heavy equipment began to roll in support of the Royal Winnipeg Rifles and the 1st Canadian Scottish. They were already advancing southward.

Jack Martin, Queen's Own Rifles

No resistance for us. When we started going through the town of Bernières-sur-Mer the residents would come out with bottles of wine, cognac, and Calvados, wanting us to stop to have a drink. There was no way we could do that, of course.

Above Left: Canadian soldiers move inland early on D-Day.

Above Right: A group of German prisoners are held captive outside the railway station at Bernières-sur-Mer

We reached the south end of the town and we had instructions that we were to go into the orchard on the left hand side, which we did. While we were there the 14th Field Regiment Artillery was on our right. They were on the right side of the road in another orchard and they were firing at an 88mm gun up on the hill. Just while we were waiting for our mortar to arrive a burst of machine gun fire came in over our heads, taking the leaves off the tree. Everybody jumped down behind a wheel of the one of the carriers there and they were stretched out. The colonel walked into the orchard and he said, "For Crissakes you don't duck for every one of them, get up!" And everybody got up sheepishly because that was the first time they had ever come under real fire. Then our armed carrier arrived and we set up the mortar. We started firing on the 88 also. I was throwing bombs down the barrel and all of a sudden the biggest explosion I had ever heard happened because the 88 had a direct hit on one of the SPs of the 14th Field Regiment. The ammunition they were carrying blew it sky high. When it did, the gun came flying over and I heard this screaming noise and I looked

Canadian troops moving artillery forward after landing on the Normandy beachhead.

around and it just caught the corner of my eye. I flattened out and that gun that must've weighed about a ton came flying past and just tipped the end of my mortar enough to knock it out of alignment. I always figured that gun had my name on it because I went right from D-Day to VE Day without being wounded. Finally we got news that the 88 had been knocked out. Now we don't know who did the actual knocking out, but we figured we had a hand in it.

An element of the German defence that caused trouble for many of the Canadian troops was the use of snipers, often firing from unknown locations.

Jim Parks, Royal Winnipeg Rifles

There was sniper fire from further in. We didn't know where it was from — we thought that some was coming from the church tower. One of our mortar crew actually hit the

Canadian soldier going through German positions on the beach and clearing them.

tower with a mortar bomb, and later on they got the tanks to fire at it. One of our chaps went in to check it out — he was told to go in and check for snipers. He got all the way to the top. But there was nobody in there.

Joe Oggy, Queen's Own Rifles

We always had trouble with the churches because up in the top of the churches they'd have an observation post, and they'd be up there. Every time we got near a church you could see the guy in the top running down in the windows. Well we always had a tank with us and the tank would just fire up there and just knock the church, and we had to start knocking all the church spires down because that's where they were hiding and they were tipping everybody off as to what we were doing down below.

Tanks moving through the narrow streets of Courseulles-sur-Mer.

Philip John Cockburn, 1st Hussars

As long as that sniper was there, our guys were getting into a pile of trouble. We got back into the tank and the crew commander said five rounds of gunfire. They'd tell you the distance — it was very close, I think five hundred yards or something — so you'd pick it up in the turret, the target that he's looking at. Five rounds, so you'd just spread them — ten o'clock … twelve o'clock … one o'clock … three o'clock … and so on. We took the guy out that was causing the infantry problems — they can make it miserable for the infantry, there's no protection there.

Further east in Mike Sector, at Courseulles-sur-Mer, the last of the German gun emplacements fell. Resisting to the bitter end, it was knocked out by a direct hit from a Royal Marines Centaur tank that had just arrived on the scene. While the town was still the site of intense street fighting, the heavy fortifications along the shoreline were silent.

While the troops on the ground pressed forward, air support continued throughout the day. Reconnaissance planes would return to their bases in England, where the aircrews would be debriefed before returning to the air.

Cec Brown, RCAF

We had the debriefing and told the intelligence people what we had seen. We would go into a room where the intelligence officers would ask for comments and bring up questions. I assume a lot of it was being used to correct any planning that wasn't working. If we criticized something because it didn't work for us, they'd look into it to see if that was the right way to approach it or if they'd have to deviate a little bit. But they were interested in getting all the opinions they could. And we were just sort of left to our own devices for the day, resting up for another go.

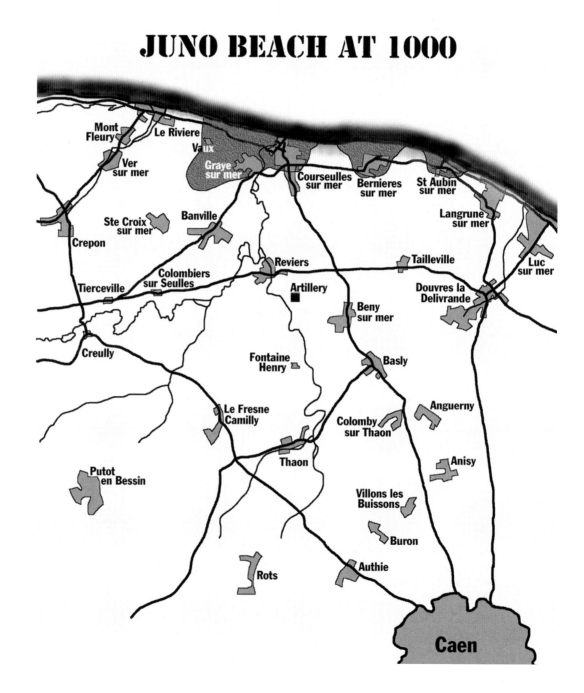

JUNO BEACH AT 1000

Every unit had three objectives for D-Day: a preliminary, an intermediate, and a final. By 1000 hours the Canadians had succeeded in capturing all preliminary objectives — the coast of Juno Beach from St. Aubin-sur-Mer to Courseulles and beyond — but the success came with a heavy price. The Royal Winnipeg Rifles suffered 128 casualties (dead and wounded), with 55 killed; the Royal Regina Rifles had 108 casualties, with 42 killed; and the 1st Canadian Scottish had 87 casualties, with 21 killed. The Queen's Own Rifles suffered the worst, with the most killed, including 7 officers, and 69 wounded. The totals were staggering, but the Canadians would not be turned away.

At 1030 hours several notable events happened simultaneously along Juno Beach. At St. Aubin-sur-Mer, the North Shore Regiment finally silenced the German emplacement and took over the town.

Frank Ryan, North Shore (NB) Regiment

> After a period of time, we had lost so many men on the beach our company commander didn't want to attack that strongpoint. We were now around it and looking towards it at the sea, and we stayed where we were until about ten o'clock. Then the message came from Tailleville where the rest of the regiment was, still fighting for the town. Colonel Buell sent a message to get moving, get it over with. So finally we all climbed over the wall and walked towards the strongpoint. Incidentally, that strongpoint was all below ground. The only thing sticking up was the rim, a piece of concrete maybe a couple of feet in diameter, and the mortar was mounted on that. That was the only thing above the ground. We walked across getting close to the trenches, and I mean very close. The Fort Garry Horse brought in one Sherman tank, which just sat up there close to the strongpoint, and they surrendered. I think

Left: The 9th Infantry Brigade arrive at Bernières-sur-Mer aboard LCI (L)s.

Right: Canadian troops on the outskirts of St. Aubin-sur-Mer. Their next destination would be Tailleville.

Below, Top Right, Bottom Right: LCI (L)s deliver the 9th Infantry Brigade to Juno Beach, where they would soon move inland to reinforce the advancing Canadian army.

there were about eighty-six or eighty-seven of them, but they were just garrison troops and I don't think they were very well trained because they could have put up one hell of a fight. They were surrounded and there was not much they could do except surrender. They didn't want to be there at night because they knew damn well that we'd burn them out or something.

Around Bernières-sur-Mer the 14th and 19th Field Regiments were engaged in combat with the Germans, while Le Régiment de la Chaudière assembled south of the town and began their advance to Beny-sur-Mer. The North Novas landed at Bernières-sur-Mer and assembled for their advance inland. In Bernières-sur-Mer the press corps had arrived, and they immediately took over the Hotel de Grave as their headquarters. Reports to the Canadian public began to originate from France for the first time in years.

North Nova Scotia Highlanders and Highland Light Infantry members heading for Normandy aboard an LCI (L).

Below Left: Arrival of the North Nova Scotia Highlanders from LCI (L) 118.

Below Right: Canadian LCI (L)s going ashore at Bernières-sur-Mer.

Don Learment, North Nova Scotia Highland Regiment

We landed at Bernières-sur-Mer at half past ten, quarter to eleven or so. We were late getting in because we couldn't go in until the landing craft were ordered in, and they were taking their orders from the high echelon. So they couldn't put us in until there was room for us. I would guess we were two and a half to three hours later in landing than we should have been, and so it took a little while to get our group together. The beaches had been secured by the people who had made the assault, and the seawall was lined with wounded, with their backs to the wall, watching us come in. We were told to dig in and wait until we could get organized a little bit, because our road in was being held up by the German 88mm. That was their all-purpose anti-tank, anti-aircraft, anti-personnel gun. In time it was taken out, then we were able to get organized. It was getting into the afternoon before we were all married up and we started inland.

The strong work of the initial landing parties made the tasks of later troops considerably easier.

The landings begin en masse. LCI (L) 299 delivers troops of the 3rd Canadian Infantry Division to the beaches just west of Bernières-sur-Mer.

John Dionne, 17th Hussars

We were the 9th Brigade — about the last ones to land. The beach was very, very quiet. The odd bomb was landing on it, but there was no excitement there. The only excitement that we had in my jeep was when I got off: I had water right up to my chin, sitting in a damn jeep and the damn thing went haywire on me and it stalled. Nobody got out, they just sat there. So I had to get out and I just waved my hands and all of a sudden I saw this tractor coming towards me. So I waited and he came to me and he said, "Here, hitch this cable onto your jeep." So he took us out. Brought us right onto the beach, and unhooked us. I figured, "I'll never get this thing started now," and so I tried it and the goddamned thing started! It was just a miracle.

Also at 1030 hours, Major General R.F. Keller, the Canadian commander in charge of Juno Beach, aboard the HMS *Hilary,* sent a communiqué to his superior, General H.D. Crerar, announcing the success of the Canadian troops: "Beachhead gained. Well on our way to our immediate objectives." All may not have gone exactly as planned, but the results were excellent.

The reserve troops were coming ashore and joining in the action. The day was still young, and there was a lot left to accomplish.

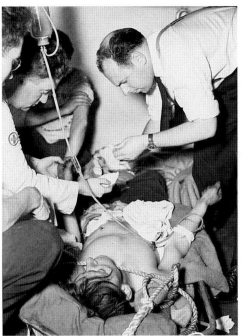

Left: Survivors of a capsized LCI being helped aboard HMCS *Prince Henry.*

Right: The wounded were taken back to the ships for treatment. Here a commando who was wounded in the early stages of the invasion is tended to by Surgeon Lieutenant John Beggs, assisted by L.S.B.A. Myers, on board HMCS *Prince David.*

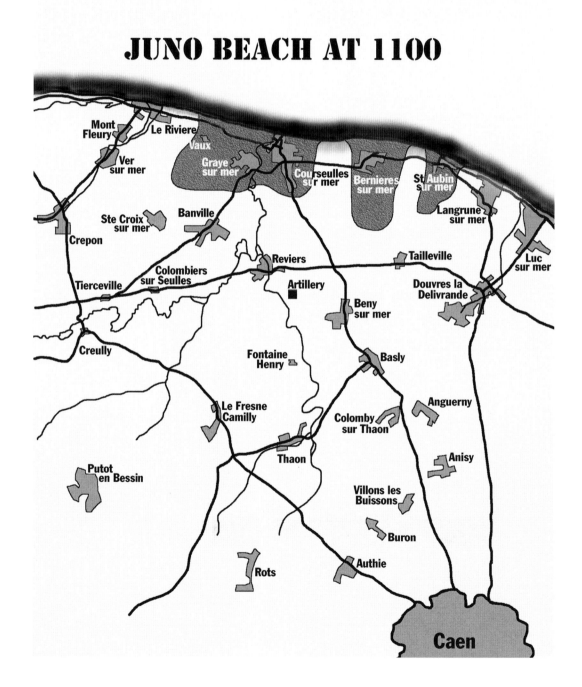

JUNO BEACH AT 1100

As the tanks arrived at Mike Sector, the remnants of the Royal Winnipeg Rifles advanced southward and cleared minefields. Despite losing three-quarters of the men in one company alone, they carried on and secured the inland villages. At that time Le Régiment de la Chaudière had advanced to the outskirts of Beny-sur-Mer, only to be held up by fierce resistance. The battle would rage until noon, with one of the bunkers getting buried (with the Germans in it) by a sapper armoured bulldozer. Once the area was cleared, Le Régiment de la Chaudière marched for Beny-sur-Mer.

Andrew Irwin, Royal Canadian Navy

We were patrolling up and down the coast. We had a British artillery officer on board who went ashore and he was our control officer. After the main bombardment, if any of the troops needed additional bombardment support, he could call back to us. At eleven o'clock on that particular morning the regiment — the Chaudières — got

Below Left: German mines all lined up on the beach.

Below Right: Landing at Bernières-sur-Mer.

View of Nan Red beach, with seawall destroyed and the ships ashore.

hung up trying to get into Beny-sur-Mer, which was about five miles inland. They were held up by three German 88mms and we were called upon to take them out. We put one salvo over and one salvo under and the next thirteen took them out.

Doug Barrie, Highland Light Infantry

The Germans had the concrete gun emplacements well sited so that they could cover the beaches from almost any angle. I know that they caused a lot of trouble and a lot of death to the attacking troops of the Seventh and Eighth Brigades. In the meantime the Queen's Own and the Chaudières had worked inland a little bit and were clearing snipers and whatnot that were left. We were very fortunate: we were probably the only regiment that didn't lose a man on D-Day itself.

Joe Oggy, Queen's Own Rifles

I remember once we were marching up a road and I had to have a bowel movement. They're all going up the road single file and I'm not going to be left out here because a sniper would pick me off. So I had to run a way up the front as far as I could then get my pants down, do my business, and get back in line again. Once a sniper picked anybody off then we'd turn right around and start firing back at the snipers because they were usually up in a tree and things like that. It was always a frightening situation — always. You never got used to it unless you went on leave. I forget how long we spent on the lines and then they took you out.

At 1120 the reserves were beginning to land. The Highland Light Infantry arrived at Bernières-sur-Mer. Once they had assembled beyond the seawall, they were to advance on bicycles that they had been issued for the invasion. This mode of transportation was easy to move, and it allowed the follow-up troops to travel quickly and catch up with the rapidly advancing front line.

Doug Barrie, Highland Light Infantry

We had three landing craft, one company on each of the three and the other company — the platoon — was split up, one platoon on each of the three boats, to balance out.

We were on the boat all the way across. We just wanted to get off the craft and get on land again. There were a lot of obstacles — they had these iron crosses in the water with mines attached to them. One of our boats hit a mine on one of them, but nobody was hurt, thank goodness. By the time we landed it was sort of high water and we got in closer than the Seventh and Eighth Brigades did — they had a longer area to cross. Our landing craft had galleries that dropped down on each side of the boat, so we just climbed down. We were just glad to get off the landing craft. We landed behind the Queen's Own at what they called Nan White sector beach on Juno. It was around 1120 when we landed.

Aerial reconnaissance photo of Bernières-sur-Mer in the late morning.

Struggling ashore with heavy gear and a bicycle.

August Herchenratter, Highland Light Infantry

As soon as we hit shore they all came up and got their bicycles and went down the ramp.

We were the second wave. The Chaudières were in there ahead in the first wave. There were a lot injured men lying there, but we had a path to go along to get to this church — that's what they told us to do.

Troops of the Highland Light Infantry and the North Nova Scotia Highlanders land at Bernières-sur-Mer.

Left: LCI (L) 125 unloading at Nan White beach.

Right: LCI (L) 299 unloading at Nan White beach.

Doug Barrie, Highland Light Infantry

Where we landed the water was just above my waist and some of the fellows were quite small and loaded down with the bikes and ammunition and their weapons and so on. If they slipped, they went under. The naval type — they had a line out to the shore and they're holding the line on shore so that you could hold onto the rope to guide yourself in. I had to pull up three or four that went under with the weight of everything — but

Left: The LCI (L) substantially increased the number of Canadian troops in Normandy.

Right: Arrival at Bernières-sur-Mer of the 9th Infantry Brigade on LCI (L) 299.

Left: View from the deck of an LCI (L) as the men of the 9th Infantry Brigade wade ashore.

Right: The reinforcements arrived with their bicycles, ready to move quickly to the front.

LCI (L) 125 delivering more troops at Nan White beach.

Above Left: The beaches became very congested as the reinforcements arrived; the exits from the beaches were not all cleared, and the rising tide reduced the amount of dry land every passing minute.

Above Right: German prisoners held by the seawall on Juno Beach.

German prisoners being guarded on the beach at Bernières-sur-Mer.

nobody drowned, thank goodness. You were still not quite knowing what to expect, whether you're going to have to fight right away or whether the landing of the Seventh and Eighth Brigades had got inland far enough that we wouldn't have to start fighting until we moved past the beaches. A lot of the wire on the seawall had been destroyed. Some by shelling and some by the engineers. A lot of the bombing seemed to be more inland — all the bombing missed the beach areas.

The major obstacle was getting off the beach. There was an awful lot of congestion. There were many wounded that were lying there, there were many dead, there were prisoners, and there was the beach party trying to get some of the tanks up the breakwater. The breakwater was about six feet high, maybe a little bigger, with wire on top of it. Because there's only one opening in the seawall near our area that we could get off, we had to queue to wait our turn. They were trying to get some of the tanks over it first. The engineers had to break that down so the tanks could get up and over it — and so we in turn could get over it. So there was a delay on the beach until they were able to do that. They were having a problem with one tank. I think it went off the side and they covered it over and went over the top of it to get the other tanks in. It was hectic there with everything going on — luckily, no firing.

Left: Tanks and armoured carriers move along the beach towards the open exits, then move inland.

Top Left: Men of the Highland Light Infantry examine the wreck of an LSI in which they came ashore on D-Day.

Top Right: The invasion was a massive undertaking, filling Juno Beach with men and material.

At 1140 hours more of the reserve units of the 3rd Division were landing on the beaches to aid in the push to the south. Shortly after that, at 1145, Major General Keller left the HMS *Hilary* and made his way to Bernières-sur-Mer to set foot on the French soil that so many Canadian had just given their lives to liberate.

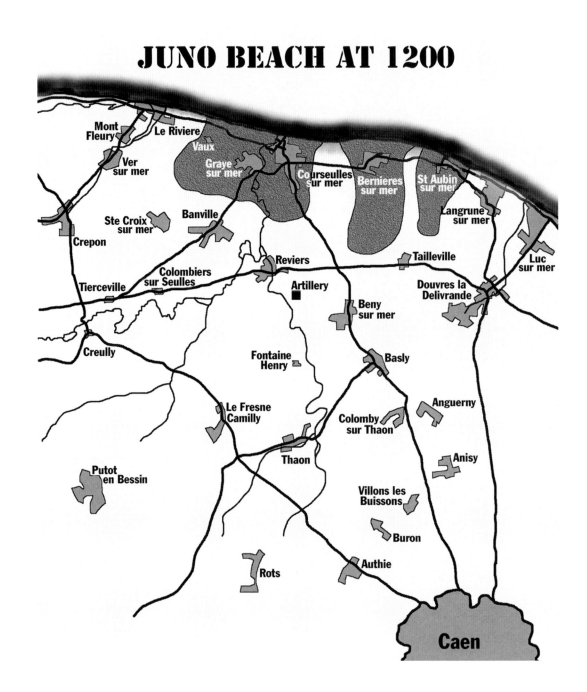

JUNO BEACH AT 1200

By noon on D-Day every unit of the 3rd Canadian Division was on shore at Juno Beach. Secured areas had been consolidated to the point that Nan and Mike sectors were linked up. The Canadians had a good foothold and were starting to move inland steadily all across the region. The last hold-out near the beaches was a German fortification situated in Courseulles-sur-Mer. It was in the southern part of the town, just beyond the château, overlooking everything from a great vantage point. It was the last obstacle before moving inland, and the Royal Regina Rifles tackled it ferociously.

To the east, the Canadian paratroopers had finally overcome the Germans at Varaville, and many of them were gathering at Le Mesnil to guard the flank. Though scattered and undermanned, the 1st Canadian Parachute Battalion had managed to accomplish all of its objectives, against considerable odds.

Left: The château at the south end of Courseulles-sur-Mer was the site of the last holdout by the Germans, and then the town was liberated. (2003)

Right: Sergeant R. Gagnon of Le Régiment de la Chaudière poses with a German POW.

Jan de Vries, 1st Canadian Parachute Battalion

> At Varaville they knocked out the machine gunners, and the snipers must have hit the officer in charge of the bunker because it was around noontime when the Germans sent out a guy with a white flag to surrender. Before that they sent out a white flag to exchange wounded and the Germans sent a cart full of their wounded down to the gatehouse and lo and behold they opened fire on it and nobody ever figured out why they did that. Anyway the firing resumed and around noontime about forty men in the bunker

An exhausted paratrooper at Varaville. The battle was long and hard, but an outnumbered Canadian unit took the objective.

Left: Four members of C Company after successfully taking the gatehouse at Varaville.

Right: The gatehouse at Varaville was a key objective for the 1st Canadian Parachute Battalion. German soldiers are being led away.

came up with their hands up. They were quite peeved when they realized there were only about twenty Canadians around them. That must have been funny. Those men that survived that battle — that is, all of their objectives had been obtained — they went to Le Mesnil, where I arrived later on that day. So that's how I got all that information first-hand when I arrived.

The 9th Infantry Brigade had landed at Bernières-sur-Mer and was moving south to reinforce the advancing unit — and to add to their forward momentum.

John Dionne, 17th Hussars

The reaction from the locals was very, very good. Of course they were damn happy to see us — mind you we weren't the first ones on, right? So I guess the reaction for the first ones on would have been a lot greater than what we had.

The continued landings at the beaches brought supplies and equipment, but the process had slowed down considerably. One factor contributing to the slowdown was the presence of Allied wrecks and German obstacles and mines in the waters offshore. Another factor — one that was becoming increasingly problematic — was congestion on the beaches.

Don Learment, North Nova Scotia Highland Regiment

There was congestion for a short time. We were very fortunate that it did not cost us the day. I really hate to think what would have happened if Rommel had been permitted to move his armour down closer to the beach as he had wanted to, but Mr. Hitler wouldn't let him do it. If they had been down close to the beaches it would have been a pretty close-run thing.

Canadian troops continued to arrive at Juno Beach throughout the day.

It was this congestion problem that caused Major General Keller dismay when he arrived at Bernières-sur-Mer at 1245. The exits from the beaches and the narrow routes leading inland had to move more quickly. Keller immediately ordered a rapid advance in order to relieve the strain. Unfortunately, by the time these orders were being implemented, the Germans had organized some resistance inland and were battling the Canadians at the front. This slowed down the progress of the Canadian units and made the rapid advance very difficult to accomplish. The success of the day was going to be determined by how much could be moved off of the beaches, as that would directly affect how far the Canadians could advance inland. At noon, it was not looking good. Those who had moved inland faced varying levels of resistance.

Left: Wrecked equipment on the beaches created more obstacles for delivering men and material to the beaches.

Right: Tank begins the advance southward from Courseulles-sur-Mer, carrying the Tricolour.

Douglas Lavoie, Fort Garry Horse

The rest of the day we were driving around the fields and supposedly heading for Caen, but we never really got that far. Nobody got that far. I think the Regina Rifles probably got the furthest, but we wouldn't have got any more than four or five miles in. We didn't meet any of the German tanks there — lucky for us. We did shoot up the odd artillery piece and trucks, but that was it. The infantry were with us most of the time. They kept their distance from us, but we knew they were there.

Jack Martin, Queen's Own Rifles

We started south on the Caen road and we passed a big battery of 75mm German guns that had been blown up. Further down the road we followed a tank. It was pretty safe to get in behind a tank. As we were going down this narrow pathway one of our riflemen had been killed and he was sitting with his back to the bank and his feet were out into the pathway. There was only room enough for a vehicle to get through and tanks just rolled over his legs and our carrier had to do the same thing. I thought, "Boy oh boy, that fella's really into the soil of Normandy." We never had time to really evaluate things and get scared or anything — we were scared but it didn't stop us from our job.

On the frontline the infantry advanced with the support of the tank units (seen on the horizon).

Back at their bases in England, when not on missions over the beaches of Normandy, the RCAF airmen kept track of the action as best they could. They found that they were able to follow the day's events not just by hearing intelligence reports but also by tuning in to public radio.

John Turnbull, RCAF

Of course it was on our radios, they were broadcasting from the beach and all. We were normally up by lunchtime and we would hear the BBC broadcasts, which would indicate a certain number of aircraft had taken off and so many were missing and what have you. Occasionally we would say,

Landing craft delivering vehicles. The supply was continuous throughout the day.

"There's a lot more missing than they're reporting." The BBC is pretty good, and for the purpose of the war tales and war reporting, they were excellent.

Bob Dale, RCAF

The BBC was exceptionally good and very well informed. You got probably as good reports coming out to the general public as we could get from our intelligence. We would hear of course more about how many aircraft were out and all that sort of thing, but you were kept right up to date. It was pretty fierce and tough for several days. They talked about the various landing areas, where the Americans went in — Omaha Beach and so on — and they'd use more vague phrases like, "They're encountering heavy resistance." They didn't talk about casualties at that stage, it was just "heavy resistance," or such-and-such being able to make advances of twenty-five miles or something like that. People got a pretty good picture and I think people realized that they were kept accurately informed; they weren't being tricked, and when the going was tough, they knew it was tough.

This hour was marked primarily by movement all across the Canadian front, as the few pockets of German resistance were overcome. In the west, the 1st Canadian Scottish met up with the Royal Winnipeg Rifles at Ste. Croix-sur-Mer, where they were facing stiff opposition in a marshy area. In an attempt to deal with the situation, an AVRE was lost as it capsized due to the unstable terrain. Eventually the resistance was overcome, and the two units continued their advance.

In the centre, Le Régiment de la Chaudière, with the tanks of the Fort Garry Horse in support, began moving into Beny-sur-Mer after overcoming some resistance en route. The remnants of the Queen's Own Rifles continued to advance in the area as well.

Having cleared the town of Courseulles-sur-Mer after a gruelling and intense battle, the Royal Regina Rifles and the 1st Hussars began to move inland towards Reviers. Despite the congestion on the beaches, the 9th also began to move inland from Bernières-sur-Mer.

Landing barges on the beach. Due to the tidal flats in Normandy, the landing craft had to have a very shallow draught when fully loaded.

Doug Barrie, Highland Light Infantry

> We didn't get off the beach until probably around one o'clock. Then we started to move inland. The French came out and they cheered us and they hugged us and they brought out whatever they had in the way of food. They wanted to give us something — whether it was cider or something else to drink. They were so glad to see us, especially if we could speak a little French and talk to them. They were so grateful that we had finally come.

JUNO BEACH AT 1300

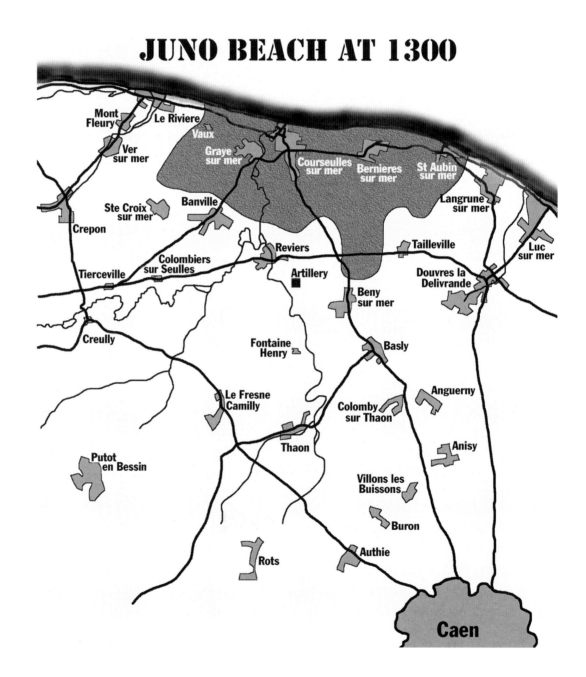

Left: The welcome was warm for the Canadian soldiers as they passed through the first liberated towns in France.

Right: Soldiers of Le Régiment de la Chaudière converse with the locals in French, much to the surprise and delight of the townspeople.

When we got through our company we got on the carrier to be taken forward and the men were trying to use their bikes, but everything was moving at such a slow pace they were walking beside their bikes.

Left: Tanks and the troops of Le Régiment de la Chaudière move through a French village on D-Day.

Right: Troops marching to the front.

August Herchenratter, Highland Light Infantry

We then got our orders and we just took off. I don't know how many miles behind the line we were from the first wave. They were in quite a long ways. When we got on our bicycles we were really clipping it off, so we caught up to them. We had a French-Canadian unit in the first wave and then when the French reserve people came out, they could get information from these people as to where the Germans were. We figured that they would be way up there, and that's why we had the bicycles.

Doug Barrie, Highland Light Infantry

We got up, and I can remember we were going through Chaudières at that time, and they were having trouble getting some snipers. There was a sniper up in one of the church towers that was giving them a lot of trouble and they finally got rid of it. They said it was a French woman that was sniping. She had a boyfriend who was in the German army. That's what I heard — I was never able to confirm that. As it turned out the bikes became rather useless and pretty well all of them were ditched along the way because we weren't moving fast enough to be able to pedal on them. They were something else to look after with all your equipment and weapons and ammunition and so on. The French civilians I think did well picking up all those bikes — they disappeared in a hurry.

Don Learment, North Nova Scotia Highland Regiment

The other companies of the North Novas: A Company was on the right riding on A Squadron, and B Company was on the left riding on B Squadron of the Sherbrookes,

Canadian troops passing through a French village, advancing as quickly as possible to gain a foothold in France.

and D Company of the North Novas followed up on the main access riding on C Squadron of the Sherbrookes. We proceeded inland. I don't think we got away from the beaches much before early in the afternoon, which put us quite a bit behind schedule.

A Canadian tank rolls through the French countryside en route to the front, bearing the Tricolour.

Without communications across the front, the Canadians' forward troops had no idea how D-Day was progressing for the British on either side of them. The concern was whether the British would advance at the same pace as the Canadians. If they did not, the Canadians' flanks would be left open. And if the Canadians advanced substantially further than the British, they would be in danger of being cut off and surrounded. The plans for D-Day were intricate, and they were devised so that all of the invading forces were interdependent when it came to covering one another's flanks. At the eastern edges of the invasion, the job of protecting the flanks lay solely with the Airborne.

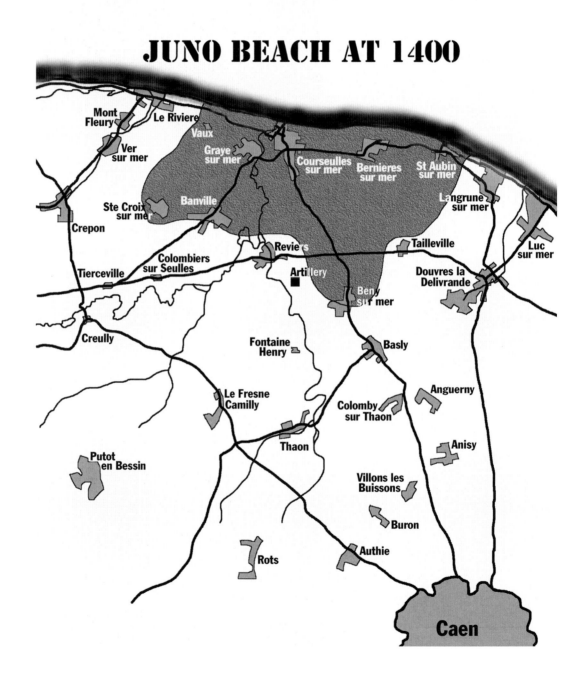

JUNO BEACH AT 1400

As the Canadian units moved south into Normandy, they met resistance of varied size and tenacity. It was a countryside of hedgerows and narrow laneways. The enemy could be hidden in a multitude of places, and the terrain was not always welcoming. It was a dangerous place to attempt a rapid advance. But when they faced resistance, the Canadians prevailed time and time again.

Joe Oggy, Queen's Own Rifles

It got to a point where the Germans didn't want to fight. They were prepared to give up. I remember one guy was standing there and one of our men had taken his wallet out and everything else and he says, "*Mein mudder, mein fadder*" — he had pictures on the floor. I said, "Pick them up," and he picked them up and put them in his pocket, that was it.

A captured German officer on D-Day.

Jack Read, Royal Regina Rifles

Most of the time the Germans would attack and counterattack. They were great at counterattacks. When we would attack a particular position, most of the time it would be slit trenches. And so we would attack that group, whatever they were — maybe a half-dozen people under cover with protection of the slit trenches. So we might chase them out of there and take up the positions, but very soon, within a matter of an hour or so, they would reorganize and they were very consistent with that particular procedure. So were we, of course. As far as an enemy is concerned, they were the most difficult in that regard.

Left: A Canadian soldier searches a German POW.

Right: The Canadian advance set a pace that the other Allied armies could not keep up with. No other country moved as far inland as Canada on D-Day.

Left: At the front there were pockets of resistance. A mortar of the Royal Regina Rifle Headquarters Company is used to combat a stubborn holdout.

Right: Wireless radio communication coordinated the actions across the front on D-Day. Here some tank crew members plot the enemy's position from information received on the radio.

Douglas Lavoie, Fort Garry Horse

The main resistance was mostly artillery, comprising mortars. The machine guns wouldn't bother us much even if they were there, and a lot of times we wouldn't even know they were there. Of course, the infantry knew they were there all the time and they did their best to do away with them.

Back at the beach — even at 1400 hours — there were still landings taking place.

Wayne Arnold, 1st Battalion Canadian Scottish Regiment

I didn't hit the beach until two o'clock in the afternoon. What happened was there were too many on board our landing craft and they took us off in Portsmouth, so I was left out of the job for the time being. But at two o'clock I came in. The beaches at Courseulles-sur-Mer were all cleared of the enemy, and there was a lot of

traffic on the beach — mostly of late personnel coming in, like myself. They were trying to clear the beaches of debris and there were all sorts of minefields and stuff that weren't too well cleared at that time. Our main objective was to get them out of the way so we could get our shipping in.

Above: M-10 tank destroyer of I Troop, 94th Battery, Anti-Tank Regiment. (l-r): Gnr. B. Long, Bgr. M.B. Farrell, Gnr. C. Henderson, Sgt. G.A. Chappel, Lt. W.E. Lee, Gnr. M. Dowhaniuk.

Left: Canadian troops continued to arrive at Juno Beach, but under far better conditions than those who arrived early in the morning.

Medical units provided essential support for wounded troops. But at mid-afternoon, most of the injuries they were seeing were minor.

The navy continued to deliver supplies to Normandy throughout D-Day as the army advanced further inland.

Left: A medic with the paratroopers gives aid to a wounded German soldier at Varaville.

Right: A field hospital was set up in this house near the paratrooper assembly area at Le Mesnil.

Ernie Jeans, 1st Canadian Parachute Battalion
I had found where the parachute field ambulance was: they were set up in a farmhouse not very far from where we were. We were so diminished in staff that the colonel told me, "You might as well go over there and work with them and see if they need any help. Any wounded that come into us, we'll send them directly there." They could do some minor operations and stabilize people and then eventually when more people came in from the beaches, a pattern was set up for evacuating the wounded.

The first people that I saw from the beach were in one of the British commando units. I think they were led by Lord Lovat. They had

landed in the British section and they had bicycles and their objective was to race ahead and join up with us.

They told me that the landing had taken place and that things seemed to be going reasonably well. At that time on that day we really didn't come under a lot of heavy fire. They were more concentrating on the beaches — and I guess they were just as confused as we were.

Our units were digging in and receiving information, trying to get as many people as we could. People were drifting into this rendezvous all the time from various other areas and trying to find out what had happened — particularly at Varaville, which was one of our big objectives.

A display of the typical medic's supplies. (Merville battery museum, 2003)

By this time people were coming in who had some slight wounds and we were trying to treat them as best we could. Most of the injuries that I saw originally were people that had injured themselves on their parachute landing, but gradually there were people coming in with gunshot wounds. I can't remember whether there were any real serious wounds that we would have to deal with because the fighting really hadn't begun yet. There were quite a few injuries with twisted ankles, and there were a couple of people who had broken ankles and broken arms from the landing that we had to immobilize and try to treat as well as we could.

John Dionne, 17th Hussars

You could be shelled like hell and to the stretcher bearers it didn't matter. They just came. They operated under fire. I just couldn't get over it. It was something amazing what these guys did. They didn't wait until the shelling stopped, they went during the firing.

As the North Shore Regiment advanced from St. Aubin-sur-Mer, they came upon the village of Tailleville. With armoured support, they captured the town.

Early in the afternoon the Royal Engineers managed to clear three exits from the beaches, which enabled more troops and supplies to move inland. At 1435 hours, Major General Keller captured the attention of the press stationed at Bernières-sur-Mer by holding his first press conference in France. It was a bold gesture, from a man who was very popular amongst his men. This was not Dieppe. It was time to show some Canadian bravado and pride.

By mid-afternoon the Royal Regina Rifles had reached Reviers, a village just west of Beny-sur-Mer. Their advancement stalled as they faced tough resistance from German anti-tank guns situated just east of the Seulles River. Meanwhile, Le Régiment de la Chaudière and the Fort Garry Horse had captured Beny-sur-Mer. Along with the Queen's Own Rifles, their thrust into Normandy was quickly gaining momentum.

Richard Rohmer, RCAF

It was about three o'clock and it was quite a different sortie from the viewpoint of what we were able to see on the ground. By this time our troops were well inland — particularly the Canadian troops, who really had moved very well. We did not see very much in terms of German activity behind the lines — we didn't see any tanks or trucks moving — which was what we were looking for. The battle was certainly on below us. The Allies were really moving in and the landing craft were continuing to come in in great volume all the way along, which indicated that a foothold had been made.

By this time, some of the congestion that had been a problem earlier was beginning to clear away, and the troops just arriving on shore were able to work their way inland.

Wayne Arnold, 1st Battalion Canadian Scottish Regiment

It didn't take us very long to move inland: the gap was all cleared. There was a little bit of activity but not a heck of a lot. A few little groups here and there as I moved inland and caught up with my regiment.

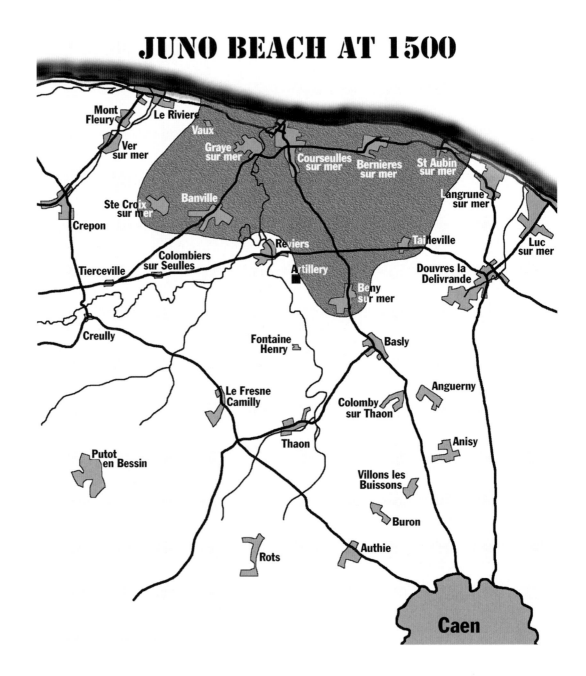

JUNO BEACH AT 1500

Canadian carriers moving inland past ongoing artillery support.

During this afternoon of Canadian victories, the men did not suffer from aerial attacks from the Luftwaffe. The dreaded German air force was a mere shadow of its former self by D-Day. The Allies controlled the skies — a decisive factor that day and throughout the Battle of Normandy. The infantry and armoured units could advance without harassment from above. In fact, they profited from close-in air support by rocket-firing Typhoons, as well as total coverage by the 2nd Tactical Air Force.

The RCAF was restricted by the range of some of the aircraft. The Spitfires could fly only so far, and for so long, although the Mustangs and Typhoons could be in the air much longer. But so great were the numbers of aircraft over the landing region that there was always immediate protection for the army at any given time.

John Turnbull, RCAF

The Luftwaffe had been disadvantaged. Very substantially. D-Day night and leading up to D-Day very few Luftwaffe aircraft were in the air. They certainly weren't in the air that night nor quite a bit of the following day. Otherwise they'd have been strafing our boys and it would have been rough. No, we had control of the skies. They had been weakened very substantially.

Ken Hill, RCAF

The Luftwaffe wasn't quite as strong as it was in the early part of the war. From reports that I've heard, they later had what they called the doodle bug and they had the rocket too — that was a pilotless aircraft that would come over and bomb indiscriminately. It would drop just anywhere in London or any particular city that they had earmarked it for.

Richard Rohmer, RCAF

I did two trips that day, one in the afternoon as well. One of our jobs going up and down the beach was to intercept if any Luftwaffe ME-109s or Focke Wulf 190s were to attack. But we didn't see any that morning or that afternoon. Some did appear and were taken on by the Spitfires, who operated much higher — they were straight fighters. They did not work for the army as we did. I'm here to tell you that I am very pleased that we didn't get bounced by German aircraft or German fighters. Our aircraft was not up to the capability of the Mustang 4: the Mustang 4 was quite different. The Mustang 1 was not a very good fighter aircraft to dogfight with the Germans. Too heavy. So we were pleased. Believe me, we had hundreds of shells fired at us by anti-aircraft guns and the stuff that we were flying through from the navy.

Above: The invasion beach was a busy centre of activity throughout the day.

Right: A Canadian convoy advancing through a French village.

Jim Parks, Royal Winnipeg Rifles

During the daytime, when the few German aircraft that did come out appeared, there'd be about five or six Spitfires chasing one Junker 88 or Messerschmitt. They were all waiting their turn to take a shot at him. They'd follow him around and get closer until finally you'd see the guy go up, and he'd flip over and he'd drop out and his parachute would barely open and he'd hit the ground. And in the meanwhile his aircraft would fly out and crash.

As the afternoon wore on, the 9th Brigade left Bernières-sur-Mer and moved south to the front. Some units had left earlier, but due to the massive congestion on the beaches and in the narrow lanes of the coastal towns, it took the better part of the afternoon for all of the 9th to move out.

Wayne Arnold, 1st Battalion Canadian Scottish Regiment

I think it was about four o'clock in the afternoon when I caught up with the rest of my unit. It wasn't too long after that we reached our D-Day objective. Moving inland wasn't very bad. There was the odd little pocket of resistance, but it didn't amount to very much. Just a few German soldiers at a time — maybe half a dozen, might be up to ten — and they were taken prisoner and looked after. We didn't have to take care of that; there were other groups there sweeping up as they went. It was just farm fields all the way inland. Plowed up from mortar bombs, gun shells, and everything

Left: G.F. Andrews of the Queen's Own Rifles at a lookout post on the front line on D-Day.

Right: The Canadian army surged forward on D-Day, exploiting the German confusion by taking large tracks of land uncontested.

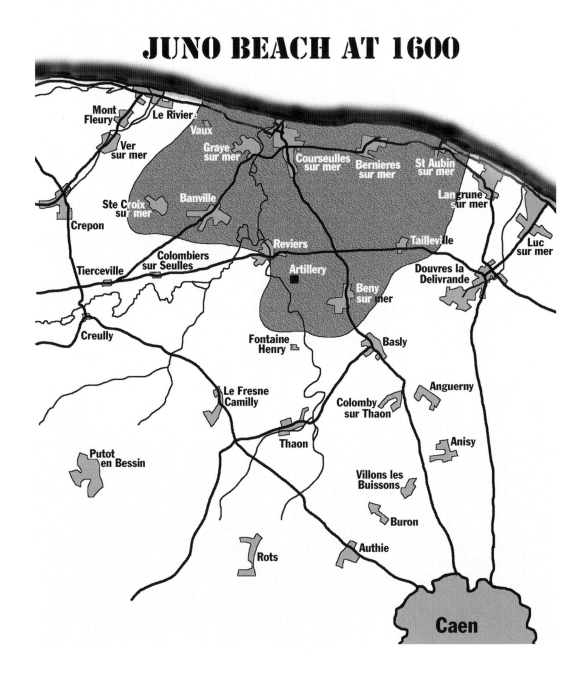

JUNO BEACH AT 1600

else. A terrific bombardment went on there early in the morning. The other men said the initial landing wasn't too bad; they were quite surprised. They expected it to be terribly rough and it wasn't too bad. It was quite amazing apparently.

The North Nova Scotia Highlanders were advancing towards Villons les Buissons, penetrating deep into Normandy. The Highland Light Infantry went to Beny-sur-Mer for the night. To the east, the Queen's Own Rifles were pushing forward to Anguerny and Anisy. To the west, the Royal Regina Rifles were making their way to Le Fresne-Camilly and Fontaine Henry. Even further west, the Royal Winnipeg Rifles and the 1st Canadian Scottish were pressing on through Tierceville and towards Colombiers-sur-Seulles. There were still several hours of daylight left, and the Canadians were pushing hard towards their objectives.

Rolph Jackson, Queen's Own Rifles

We didn't run into the Free French — they were there further inland. They were blowing railroads, causing disruption any way they could. Some of them were getting caught and executed — they weren't treated as prisoners of war when they were taken.

Unloading operations at Juno Beach on D-Day

With limited resistance from the German Luftwaffe, the RCAF found themselves focusing on the action down below — sometimes observing, sometimes attacking.

Cec Brown, RCAF

At one point I recall a hedgerow and seeing German troops bent over going along the hedgerow and Canadians going down the other side — they were going to meet at the corner. The temptation was to go down and blast the Germans but we had one job and one job only and it was to patrol the beach and keep enemy aircraft out. Typhoons had that other responsibility if we have ground targets. And just while we were watching about a half a dozen Typhoons came in and I think they were firing rockets and they went in and they blasted the hell out of that hedge and people.

Doug Barrie, Highland Light Infantry

It wasn't 'til late that day that several Germans came around strafing. I can remember two that strafed us around Beny-sur-Mer — but they didn't stay around long, they were just flying low and fired off their machine guns and were away.

A dead Nazi soldier in a trench after a Canadian assault. Some held out until the bitter end, while many Ost troops looked for a quick end to their involvement in the war by surrendering.

Cec Brown, RCAF

Troops that were getting in, we could see them coming, quite often assisted by American Thunderbolts and our Typhoons. They'd go in and blast the defences — they're pretty visible so they had no trouble there, and those rockets that the Typhoons carried were devastating. They'd tear a tank apart. We say we stayed at the beach area but we were in the vicinity. We widened the patrols a little bit to make sure that enemy aircraft wouldn't be bothering our guys that had got in there. You could see that there was some fighting going on, but details were not that easy to recognize. They were still coming in, pouring troops in.

Richard Rohmer, RCAF

Among the things that we saw as we came back to England that afternoon were these great, huge concrete blocks. Huge, enormous things being towed out of port across to the beach. We didn't know what they were. We had seen them being constructed for many, many weeks and of course they turned out to be pieces of the mobile port called Mulberry. One of the things that Dieppe indicated to the strategists and the planners was that we would not be able to take a port by frontal attack. And in order to supply an army and to keep supplying it with men, equipment and supplies, oil, gas, whatever you need — you had to have a port. It had to be there almost instantly, and so that's why the Mulberry ports were created.

JUNO BEACH AT 1700

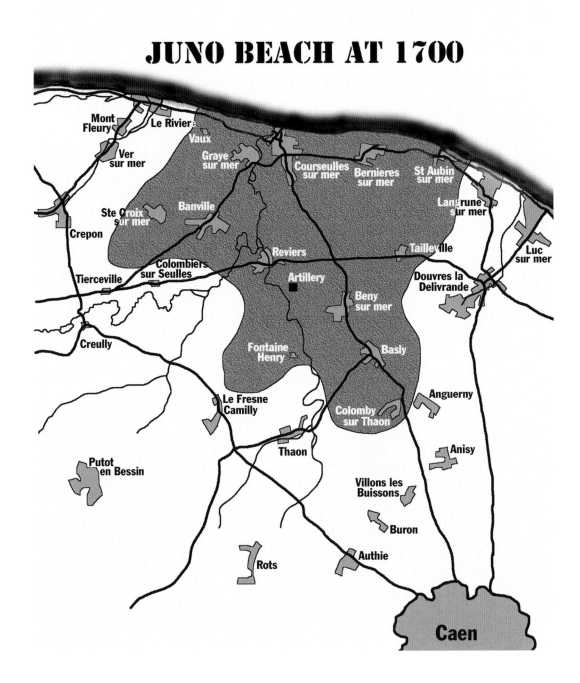

Despite the success of the invasion, only one Allied unit actually achieved all of its overall objectives for D-Day. This was Canada's 1st Hussars, who captured the Caen-Bayeux highway intersection late in the afternoon.

Philip John Cockburn, 1st Hussars

We carried on to Carpiquet airport. That was our objective for that day, and that's where we got to. It was about twelve kilometres from the water to this airport. We didn't feel very good about that because we had no tanks. We thought, "What can we do? We can go as far as we can, and when they start to fight us, we'd better stop." You look around you and you don't see too much help. It wasn't there. We stayed around the airport — it must have been at least three days. It was something we were just trained to do, and we did it without hesitation and without even being afraid. There were pockets of resist-

Left: Some German prisoners were used to help move the wounded and do other chores.

Right: The Royal Winnipeg Rifles march through the fields of Normandy. Although their ranks were severely depleted that morning, they did not hesitate to lead the advance on D-Day.

Left: A German POW captured during the assault on Juno Beach.

Right: German POWs marching across Juno Beach and heading for transportation to England, where they would spend the rest of the war in POW camps.

ance. That evening it was just like the sun was coming up as our planes bombed the front. I think all together on the whole front, not just on our front, there were something like 4,800 bombers — so that's a lot of power. We were more concerned about the water, but for some reason we weren't ever afraid at any time. We just thought it was another get-together, but it was for real, that was the only difference then.

Colombiers-sur-Seulles was also captured to the west, where the 1st Canadian Scottish and the Royal Winnipeg Rifles joined forces and began creating defensive positions for the evening. Some Canadian units advanced so far that they had to be called back to avoid exposing their flanks. In the waning hours of daylight, Canada's units started to dig their slit trenches and secure their positions along the front line.

The paratroopers continued their mission, cutting off German routes of transit as they moved towards the rendezvous point at Le Mesnil.

Left: Colombiers-sur-Seulles was one of the farthest reaches into France of the Canadian forces on D-Day.

Right: The village of Colombiers-sur-Seulles.

Jan de Vries, 1st Canadian Parachute Battalion

Eventually we got to where we were supposed to be — the crossroads called Le Mesnil. Everybody was to head for the high ground — Le Mesnil — to form our defence line. B Company and C Company had already been in to take the DZ, protect the pathfinders, blow the bridge over the Divette, tackle the German headquarters in Varaville, knock out the German strongpoint, and blow out a German signal station.

It must have been about five o'clock in the afternoon when we finally got there. We broke away, and the men went to the companies where they were supposed to go. I went to my C Company and there weren't a lot of guys there. They were scattered all over the place — I wasn't the only one.

My first job when I arrived — I thought — was to dig in. A few of the guys from my platoon were dug in behind a hedge, aimed across a farmer's field. I was told to dig in at the side of a farmer's road so I could keep my eye on that road. I picked my spot and threw a lot of my gear down there, and then they said go find the Germans. I went on the field side of that hedge, got about halfway along, and there was one of our fellows — a sniper lying with his rifle aimed at that bush across the field. I wondered what he was doing there instead of being back with our line. When I went up and said something, nothing happened, and when I went to step over him I was surprised that he didn't move, so I stopped and shook him and he had a bullet right through his forehead. Some German sniper must have seen him first. I hurried up, crouched a little lower in case the sniper was still around. I don't know how long I was walking — I know I crossed some fields, checked through some hedges to see if the road was clear. Eventually I came to a fairly thick hedge that was outside a gravelly road and I was going to cross it. But looking through that hedge there was a

Above Left and Right: Members of the 1st Canadian Parachute Battalion who were taken prisoner on D-Day.

Left: Exhausted paratroopers late on D-Day. They had been up all day on June 5 preparing, had flown over the Channel at midnight, and had fought through the night as they achieved their objectives.

Left: Paratroopers dug-in near Le Mesnil, protecting the eastern flank of Operation Overlord.

Right: A Canadian para-trooper, an RCAF flight officer, and a British glider pilot at an assembly point in Normandy.

farmhouse about three hundred feet away from the road. There were a lot of Germans milling around so I said, "Well, that's where the Germans are." I headed back, reported in to the captain who had taken over the company — Captain Hansen. I showed him on a map where the house was, and that information went back to the navy, who was our artillery at that time.

I was digging in a little bit later when I heard this whistling sound — the first time I ever heard it. It turned out it was these big navy shells. On a patrol a few days later, we passed that place and there was hardly anything left of that house. It was all huge craters all around it. The navy was bang on.

1800

As the adrenalin from the day of combat began to wear off, the men began to feel the pangs of hunger. Due to seasickness on the trip over, and intense fighting and marching throughout the day, many of the men had not eaten in twenty-four hours. Others who had eaten food on the ship had likely been unable to keep it down during the rough ride in to the beaches. The men began to become concerned about something other than Germans.

Doug Barrie, Highland Light Infantry

As we got to Beny-sur-Mer it was about suppertime and we were told that we would be spending the night there and to take up defensive positions to be ready for a counterattack. There was a big château there with high walls. We punched holes through the wall and dug slit trenches behind it so that we could have cover and also fire out.

Gunner W.G. Magee on guard duty during the D-Day invasion.

Below: Four paratroopers relaxing after a tense day.

Wilf Delaurie, 1st Canadian Parachute Battalion

We had our emergency packs. We ate compo pack, as we called it; it wasn't the best but it was food and we were hungry.

Ernie Jeans, 1st Canadian Parachute Battalion

Most of the time it was just eating these biscuits and sardines. Got sort of sick of eating biscuits and sardines, but at least it kept you going.

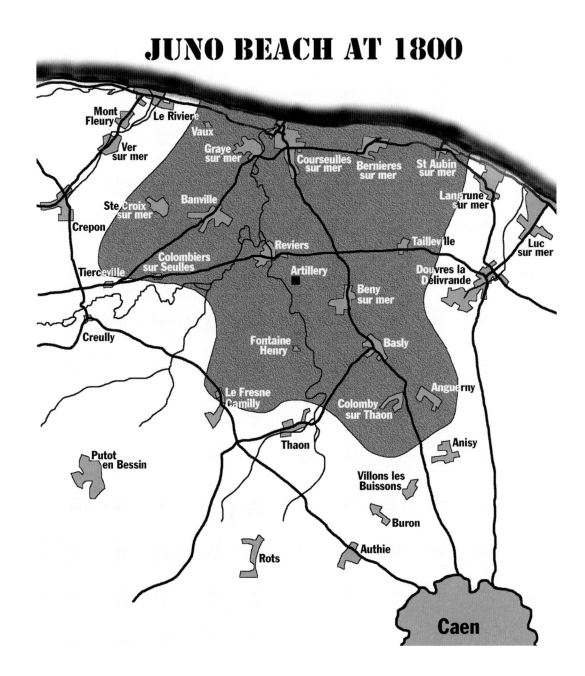

JUNO BEACH AT 1800

Left: Two paratroopers in a foxhole, prepared for action with a mortar.

Right: Tailleville was home to German command for the area, and resistance was heavier than elsewhere inland.

At 1830 hours, the 9th Brigade advanced through the captured towns of Tailleville, Basly, and Colomby-sur-Thaon and dug in. Le Régiment de la Chaudière was settling in there for the night. The Highland Light Infantry was stationed at Beny-sur-Mer. The advance was slowly coming to a halt for D-Day, and the Canadians were preparing defensive positions for a possible German counterattack that night or the next morning.

The town of Tailleville.

Frank Ryan, North Shore (NB) Regiment

They had Tailleville pretty well taken care of, and we moved on to what they called the radar station. Apparently that controlled all of the radio traffic for the whole of that area. We put in an attack on that, and couldn't get anywhere, and the British 51st Division came along. This cocky officer said, "We can take care of that for you," and he got on his radio and said to send up some M-10 tanks. They started towards

A Canadian tank rolls through a French village.

the radar station and *bang-bang*, they knocked them all out. So we got word then that we were going to bypass it and we left and kept going. I think the British surrounded it and just sat there and they didn't take it until it was surrendered quite a bit of time later. We stayed all night at Tailleville near the radar station, on the road.

But while the action for the day had come to a near halt for many, others were still seeing counterattacks from German troops.

Tank battle in front of the 9th Infantry Brigade HQ.

Jan de Vries, 1st Canadian Parachute Battalion
The Germans put in an attack from the field that I had gone across — they were firing at us from the hedge at the far end of the field. Then they set up their machine gun and rifle fire. Everybody in our group all of a sudden started opening up on them, and that was a mistake because as soon as we did that the Germans stopped firing and disappeared. Now they knew where we were and that's all they wanted to know. From then on we got shelled and mortared every damn day.

Wilf Delaurie, 1st Canadian Parachute Battalion
There were small actions, very small, and some companies might get hit and other companies might not. Gradually what happened during the day and the next two or three days was our strength increased because we had the stragglers like myself who didn't meet up with any columns of our own guys. I was sort of still apprehensive as to what was coming. Mortar fire was coming in and you never knew when it would come. We were on edge a bit but we were in a good fighting mood.

With only one final objective having been met on June 6, it appeared that the planners of D-Day had been a little too ambitious.

August Herchenratter, Highland Light Infantry

Some of the Canadian tanks got almost as far as Villons les Buissons and then the German 88s just clobbered them. They had mobile 88s on a big tractor-trailer that they could tow anywhere. They had three kinds of shell: ack-ack for planes, another that was shrapnel, and one solid one that would go in one side of the tank and out the other side. They were powerful. We captured one of them that was on their tractor-trailer — beautiful looking thing.

The Royal Regina Rifles reached Fontaine Henry and stopped for the evening. They were barely halfway to their planned objective for D-Day, but no one had anticipated the sort of resistance they had faced at Courseulles-sur-Mer and outside of Reviers.

Le Fresne-Camilly was one of the deepest forays into France for Canadian troops on D-Day.

Jack Read, Royal Regina Rifles

I was outside of Reviers, a little bit inland — that's where we spent the first night. On that night we were positioned in and around the towns

JUNO BEACH AT 1900

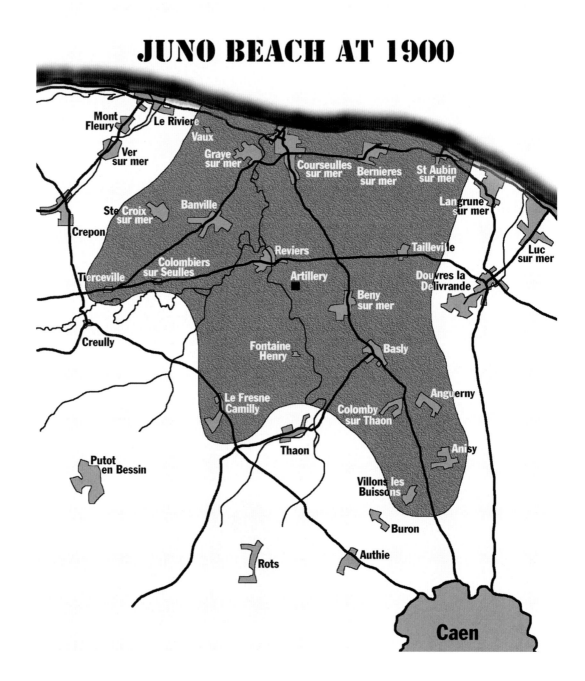

Mont Fleury
Le Riviere
Vaux
Ver sur mer
Graye sur mer
Courseulles sur mer
Bernieres sur mer
St Aubin sur mer
Ste Croix sur mer
Banville
Langrune sur mer
Crepon
Reviers
Tailleville
Luc sur mer
Tierceville
Colombiers sur Seulles
Artillery
Douvres la Delivrande
Beny sur mer
Creully
Basly
Fontaine Henry
Anguerny
Le Fresne Camilly
Colomby sur Thaon
Thaon
Anisy
Putot en Bessin
Villons les Buissons
Buron
Rots
Authie
Caen

and spent the night. I and my group were sent by the commanding officer over to our left to contact one of our sister regiments. That happened during the night, and by morning we were back in position and ready to start off again.

John Dionne, 17th Hussars

We followed the regiment, and the first night when we bedded down, we all bedded down in a dried-up ditch. We didn't do any digging of trenches or anything. We weren't right at the front; we were still following. We never got up there. We

Left: The town of Le Fresne-Camilly. (2003)

Right: Men of the Royal Regina Rifles, D Company, holding their position on the front line.

Fontaine Henry was on the front line as D-Day came to a close.

Left: The château at Fontaine Henry. (2003)

Right: The church at Fontaine Henry. (2003)

The Canadian forces faced fields and pastures throughout Normandy on their advance. The wide hedgerows around these fields presented difficult and dangerous strategic positions to approach. They made excellent defensive positions for the Germans who were dug in there. (Fontaine Henry, 2003)

had a good night's sleep. The odd plane was flying over, but it didn't bother us at all. We weren't being shelled; it was very quiet. We spent the night there at Villons les Buissons.

Some managed to advance as far as Le Fresne-Camilly, and the day was still a success. The 9th Brigade continued to move south to Anguerny and Authie, where they would stop for the night.

Canadian soldiers N.L. Garrant and G.K. Gree dig a slit trench.

Don Learment, North Nova Scotia Highland Regiment

There wasn't a lot of opposition and we got quite far inland before darkness set in and we were ordered to settle in for the night. During the evening the troops of Kurt Meyer's SS people made quite an attack over to our left. Actually I'm told they cut right through to the beach but they were afraid they were going to be cut off so they returned to where their own lines were. But in that attack they wounded both the company commander and the second-in-command of D Company on our left. I've read and been told that our group got further inland on D-Day than any other group that had landed by sea. Now I don't know whether that's true or not. The paratroopers certainly got further in than we did, but they jumped the night before. We got in a long piece for the first day.

Doug Barrie, Highland Light Infantry

Canadian soldier on guard.

The North Novas got the furthest inland because they got down past Buron and into Authie. I guess most of them spent the night in Buron, but at that time the 12th SS had not arrived on the scene and they had a quiet night before moving forward at first light the next morning. Artillery was on the move up, moving forward, so they could give closer support. Being on the move, they couldn't do any firing. There was I think a forward observation officer — a "FOO" they called them — with the North Novas but he couldn't call down fire because of them being on the move. Unfortunately the British on our left got stalled and the British on our right got stalled. What happened is our brigade kept going up there in a straight line just like a finger and there was nothing in support on either side.

Wayne Arnold, 1st Battalion
Canadian Scottish Regiment

Canadian troops lie low during the D-Day action.

Our objective for the day was Putot-en-Bessin — a railroad crossing. We'd been assigned to take that and stop all rail traffic. Our regiment was in a rear position — you see there were two forward and one rear. It wasn't too exciting. Of course, maybe I'm not the excitable type.

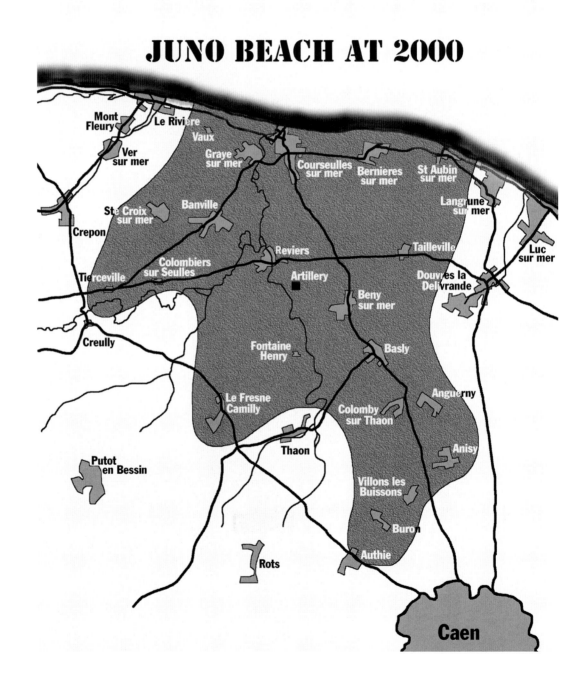

JUNO BEACH AT 2000

As the last light of the day faded, those Canadian units that hadn't already dug in for the night were about to. The North Nova Scotia Highlanders and the Sherbrooke Fusiliers (27th Armoured Regiment) battled their way into Villons les Buissons and Anisy. It was late in the day when they overcame the mortar and anti-tank fire to capture the towns. The surviving members of the Queen's Own Rifles were at Anisy, as well as at Aguerny. They were a mere five kilometres away from Carpiquet airfield, a D-Day objective that was well fortified. They were ordered to move back and secure their positions. That night, the men prepared for attacks that would not come. The Germans were in disarray and unable to react effectively. The element of surprise had worked heavily in the Allies' favour, and the German plan to turn back the invasion at the beaches had failed miserably. They were beset by confusion and a failure in their chain of command.

2000

Charles McNabb, Queen's Own Rifles

> We advanced straight up to the Carpiquet airport and then had to pull back because the bunkers were in Carpiquet, and our regiment had advanced further than any other outfit, leaving our flanks wide open. We dug in and we were waiting for a counterattack.

Top Left: The town of Villons les Buissons was another position taken and secured by the Canadians on the evening of June 6, 1944. (2003)

Top Right: The town of Anisy. Note the poster advertising the opening of the Juno Beach Centre on June 6, 2003.

Bottom Right: Anisy. The walled-in roadways posed a hazard of possible ambushes without cover. (2003)

Joe Oggy, Queen's Own Rifles

> We settled down for that night, digging slit trenches, and then food came up to us at nighttime and we ate what we could. The smartest thing the Canadian army ever did

Left: R.G. Brodie of the Queen's Own Rifles stands guard on the front line.

Right: Digging in for the night in Normandy. Slit trenches were difficult to dig thanks to the hard, chalky ground in Normandy.

was give us a full-length shovel — a regular shovel like you have today — and a pick. They were much better than the little army things the Americans had — you could get nowhere with those. One man would carry a shovel in his webbing at the back and the other man would carry a pick. The shovels came in very handy because you could dig in a hurry. We didn't meet the enemy head-on — I don't know where in the hell they were — but we dug in quickly to get down. You could get your head in — you always looked after your head and other parts that were important to you.

Men of Le Régiment de la Chaudière holding their position in a slit trench.

August Herchenratter, Highland Light Infantry
We got up to Villons les Buissons, about two miles from Buron, and packed all the bicycles up. The anti-tank people would put the bikes on their tanks, and if they had a day where they had to go for some water, they'd go bicycle for their water. Then we waited. We were parked there for pretty near a month. When we dug in that night there was a German that came over and he thought he heard something and thought maybe there were some other Germans there. We got a hold of him. We knew that we weren't too far behind the enemy.

Left: The Canadians dig in at Villons les Buissons on the evening of June 6. It would become a hotly contested village within the next few days. (2003)

Right: The town of Villons les Buissons. (2003)

While we were at Villons les Buissons, I went on a night patrol and we got as far as the anti-tank ditch. We were listening and could hear them talking — we'd come across a lot of dugouts that they were in.

Doug Barrie, Highland Light Infantry

Nobody could sleep and nobody wanted to sleep. Really — we were dead tired and we were sick, too. We hadn't slept coming across and most of us hadn't eaten and couldn't hold anything down and most of us acquired headaches and so on. But there's no sleep. Everybody had to keep on their toes that night and I had to go around from slit trench to slit trench to keep them awake because they got so tired. The tendency was to fall asleep and you needed two men per slit so you had to make sure at least one was awake. I know I didn't get any sleep, I think I may have got six hours of sleep in the first week. It got so that I was so tired and exhausted that if I'd lean up against a tree I'd drop right off.

A group of Canadian soldiers stop for a quick meal. Many of them had not eaten in twenty-four hours, or had lost their meals to seasickness.

You had to keep yourself going — there was much more for an officer to do. We had O groups, we had to see if they got their food and everything else, keep them informed, keep them doing things. But the men — it was hard on them because they

Corporal J.W. Bennett of the Queen's Own Rifles inspects a pile of haversacks.

A Canadian soldier on watch, with a French village in the distance.

often didn't know what the heck was going on, what was up ahead, and when we'd be in action and when we'd have to fire and if they'd counterattack. It was a very edgy time.

Jim Parks, Royal Winnipeg Rifles

The daylight hours were long. We dug in about three or four places, and it was hard to dig in. It was chalk — you could only get in a few inches. So you'd get ready to move and we'd move. Why we moved, I don't know, but there were a lot of shells and anti-aircraft fire because the Jerrys were coming over and dropping bombs.

Douglas Lavoie, Fort Garry Horse

We got something to eat as best we could — the rations that we carried in the tank. Then we posted a guard, and of course decided who was going to be guard for a certain time. We would have one man on guard all night out of that crew, so we'd break it up into slots — I'll do this and you'll do that and Charlie will do this and we had it all figured out. That's the way it went, nothing very exciting.

We ate as fast as we could and we fell asleep as fast as we could. We'd sleep in the tank for that first night. The driver and the co-driver each had their own seat. It would be a little more uncomfortable in the turret because there were three fellows up there — the gunner and the radioman and the crew commander. It was only that first night, and we always had somebody outside the tank on guard in a hidden position. You don't pace around there like in front of Buckingham Palace. You get in a spot where you can watch and are able to warn the crew. After that we had other ways of sleeping at night by digging a trench and driving the tank over the top of the trench and sleeping in there. Some of us would sleep in the tank, too.

As darkness descended on Normandy, a wide stretch of land six to ten miles deep was controlled by the Canadian forces. Despite the fierce resistance at the landing beaches and in the coastal towns, the Canadians had accomplished a great deal and had advanced further than their British and American counterparts.

Fatigue began to catch up with many of the soldiers. But while some slept, others stayed awake — either because they were keeping watch or because the excitement of the day made sleep impossible.

Joe Oggy, Queen's Own Rifles

Very wary — very careful. What we did in my section — you're one hour on and then you'd wake the next guy up in the next slit trench and then he'd have to stand up for an hour. All night long everybody had to take turns staying awake. You had to be careful. What I used to do at dusk, I'd say, "Now look — see that little bush," and the wind would be blowing it, "as it gets darker that'll look like a whole platoon of men marching, so don't fire at it because you're going to wake everybody up and we've got to have our sleep." I did that with every man in my section. The wind would blow it and at nighttime you'd swear somebody was coming at you. It was a pretty hair-raising situation all the time — especially at nighttime. Then alongside of us they would fire tracer bullets and that was for our planes up above. These planes would drone over. These bullets would wave the guns up and down and these tracers would be a laneway for their planes to drop their bombs down at night.

Ernie Jeans, 1st Canadian Parachute Battalion

Having been keyed up all the day before and that evening on the planes, it wasn't until evening of D-Day itself that we started to feel a little weary. We lay down and had a sleep for a little while and then woke up again. Our task was to hold these positions — we were the left flank of the invasion army. I think when you land and you have a job to do, you don't really think of a larger scope of things — at least I didn't. I was quite worried about the fact that if the doctor and the rest of our medical organization didn't show up, what really would I have to do? I had a fair amount of training, but I certainly wasn't a doctor. He didn't show up and I was left to look after the wounded and comfort the dying. It was a very traumatic experience — I wasn't really prepared for what was going to happen.

R.A. Marshall points out a hole in his steel helmet that was made by a German sniper during the landing on the beach.

Douglas Lavoie, Fort Garry Horse

We had been going all day, firing the guns at very distant targets — trucks and guns. Looking back on it, none of us really knew until the next morning that we had lost thirteen men. Nobody in our tank knew, because we were the second unit through the seawall, right after Major Brey's unit of the Fort Garry Horse had gone through. Our time there was spent getting through the hole in the seawall and driving through the little town of St. Aubin. The rest of the time was spent almost by ourselves, just going ahead and shooting at things that were enemy guns or trucks and things like that.

For still others, it was hunger and illness that kept them awake.

Joe Oggy, Queen's Own Rifles

I had the runs badly. I had been eating green apples because of the hunger, and of course too many green apples and you know what happened. So what cured me was their fresh bread. In the town there was a bakery and they had these little hedges all around their properties, so I crept along the hedges all the way through into the bakery. We had landing money, we had French francs printed specially for that, and I don't know how much they gave us — fifty, I think. I bought some fresh bread and I was eating this soft bread and it cured me. I did that two nights in a row, crawling back in there to get it. Nobody bothered me because these hedges were wide and high so it was a good place to crawl. I always brought this bread back and ate it. It cured my stomach.

Out in the Channel, the Canadian navy patrolled, wary of German attacks by sea.

Andrew Irwin, Royal Canadian Navy

We continued to sweep, and then our duty, once darkness came, was to go outside the landing area and do anti-submarine patrol. At the same time we had to watch out for German E-Boats, which were stationed in Le Havre. They were like motor torpedo boats or motor gunboats and were very, very fast.

We never saw any E-Boats, but some others on the patrol at night did. We had a couple of run-ins with aircraft coming over and randomly dropping bombs. We had a couple of sonar echoes that we depth-charged, but in that particular area there were so many wrecks around you never knew whether you had a live one or not.

On shore, the men settled into their slit trenches and prepared for the Germans. It was inevitable that there would be a counterattack and an attempt to push the Allies back into the ocean. It was just a question of when.

Hungry, exhausted, and in shock from the intense combat, the men faced a night of uncertainty. The invasion had begun brutally, but after the initial action it had progressed well, and the operation had been a success. But while the Allies had a foothold in Europe, that foothold was tenuous, and there was still a risk of being driven back by a blitzkrieg attack. They needed to push further into France. To savour the victory of the day would be premature and dangerous. For the Allied troops, the fight had just begun.

Jan de Vries, 1st Canadian Parachute Battalion

I don't remember feeling hungry or tired until I started to dig in late at night. That's when it started to hit me. I had an emergency pack, and when I had part of my slit trench dug I stopped and had something to eat out of my kit. I didn't finish my slit trench until after that first barrage — that woke me up to the fact that I had better get a little deeper. So I went at least four feet deep. I even hollowed out a little bit out of the bank just a little bit so I could squeeze over because then I knew that shrapnel could come straight down at me.

A paratrooper on guard in a wooded area. With the darkness came the anticipation of a German counterattack. It did not come that evening.

When the first explosion took place it was deafening. Then it got worse. I could hear this damn shrapnel flying all around and that's the first time I heard this whizzing noise. I heard them called whiz-bangs. Some pieces of shrapnel will actually spin like a propeller and I don't know what causes it, but all of a sudden they just go *zip* straight down. I guess it's the fragmentation that takes place — some

Display of a paratrooper's kit and weapons. (Merville battery museum, 2003)

pieces maybe take a certain form and act like that. That's what made me hollow out the side of my trench a little bit. But that was a pretty frightening sensation to go through that first barrage.

Francis Godon, Royal Winnipeg Rifles

So we dug in a few places the first night and we captured a bunch of Germans ourselves. A patrol came at night — we never moved until they got right up on us. We just put the flares and there they were, and we all jumped up with our rifles and they just dropped everything and got their hands up. We kicked some butts and brought them back. And so we fought all night. We had to try and blow the railroad track so they wouldn't come in with more men. I think it was C Company that came in and helped us because we were short. The thing was not to let the Germans know that we had that many casualties. We had to keep pretending that we were still in full force.

Frank Ryan, North Shore (NB) Regiment

There were so many casualties, and we had no reinforcements for quite some time. The reinforcements we did get weren't very well trained. They did the best they could, but it seemed that you'd lose more reinforcements than the originals.

Jan de Vries, 1st Canadian Parachute Battalion

The guys could see enough when they were on at night. In France in those days you could see the trees across the field in the dark — just an outline. I don't know how many times you could swear you could see troops coming at you in the dark. It took me almost ten years to learn to sleep with my eyes closed.

During the last hour of that momentous day, the Canadian presence was felt enormously. Infantry, artillery, and armoured units held the front lines. Paratroopers guarded the flank to the east. And the air force was preparing for another evening of bombing the Germans. The RCAF, with its bombers, fighters, and reconnaissance aircraft, would hinder the advance of the German response to the invasion and soften the defences along the front line. The Canadian navy protected the newly captured beaches as well as the transport ships that were constantly delivering more supplies to fuel the advance further into German-occupied France. D-Day was a magnificent team effort. There had never been anything like it before in history. And the men who experienced it hoped that it would never have to happen again.

Ed Reeve, Armoured Corp HQ

> The day ended with shells going over. I know I didn't get any sleep. There was no day-end, it was just a continuous twenty-four hours of go-go-go.

**Arthur Perry, 7th Canadian
Infantry Brigade**

> We woke up in the middle of the night and all I could see was tracers going through the air, and fellas were digging holes in a hurry to get underground.

**Don Learment, North Nova Scotia
Highland Regiment**

> I've never seen such a sight — I would call it a night of fireworks or pyrotechnics — in all my life. It was coming up from all of the ships and the beaches. There were a few German aircraft around, and they were lit-

Canadian soldiers in silhouette against search lights at night.

erally blown to pieces or driven off by the anti-aircraft fire of all the fleet and whatever anti-aircraft was ashore. It was absolutely unbelievable.

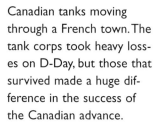

Canadian tanks moving through a French town. The tank corps took heavy losses on D-Day, but those that survived made a huge difference in the success of the Canadian advance.

Douglas Lavoie, Fort Garry Horse

Before we went into action, all of the Allied tanks had this huge white star painted on the top of them. There were other means of identification. If you needed help from the air force, we had different coloured flares and we also had sheets that we spread on the ground with different colours, which had a language that the air force knew of. We used the Typhoons a lot and we never had an accident with them, like them bombing us instead of the other guys. A lot of Typhoon guys didn't come through. I talked to a Typhoon pilot and he said that the Typhoon was probably the worst plane that they could ever have chosen for that kind of a job. It had such a powerful motor in the thing and it had this terrible thrust — it was almost learn by experience, and some of the fellows never had a chance to learn. They never pulled up because they never knew when to start pulling out. We never saw that, all of our Typhoon pilots were experienced and they did their job — a great job.

Canadians asleep on an invasion craft on D-Day. Few started the day with adequate sleep, and for those on the front line, it would be a very long week without proper rest.

Jan de Vries, 1st Canadian Parachute Battalion

It wasn't what you would call a very successful airborne operation, but everything happened all right, and everything was carried out. There's a lot that depends on luck, and circumstances in war are always favourable to those with the most initiative.

Rolph Jackson, Queen's Own Rifles

I was walking wounded because I was only hit in the hand. I was sent to the MO somewhere around midnight as the company was moving into their area where they were to dig in, up between Anguerny and Anisy — what we called Hill 80. We got back to the hospital on the ninth and got evacuated fairly quickly. People would come in wanting first-hand information and you'd tell them what happened. They'd say, "Oh, we can't print that! Can't get by the censors." "Okay, you want BS, that's what you got," and that's what was published in the paper a good many early days of the war. They wouldn't let them tell the truth. They wouldn't tell that we got wiped out. And we did.

END OF DAY

As June 6, 1944, drew to a close, Operation Overlord was being called a success. Surprise had been achieved, and the Allies had obtained a foothold in Europe. More than 155,000 troops had landed (21,400 of them Canadian), along with thousands of vehicles and 4,000 tons of supplies. The Atlantic Wall had been breached, and the Germans' failure to drive the invasion back into the sea, much less to effectively mount a counterattack, spelled their eventual doom in the Second World War.

It was a day of destiny, one that Canada figured in prominently. The resistance at Juno Beach was second only to that at Omaha Beach, and the ratio of casualties sustained by the Canadians in the first wave was quite comparable to that of the Americans.

Overall, on June 6, 1944, there were 340 Canadians killed, 574 wounded, and 47 taken prisoner. But the sacrifices were made for a just cause. No other war was so necessary, and no battle more pivotal. With an enemy as evil as the Nazi regime, there was only one acceptable outcome. Anything less than victory would have been disastrous for the world. D-Day was only one day in a war that lasted nearly six years, but it is the day that shall always be remembered. For those brave Canadians who were there, who participated, who took an active part in determining the course of history, we should all be thankful.

Left: Andrew Irwin. (2003)

Right: William Kelly. (2003)

Andrew Irwin, Royal Canadian Navy

I feel honoured to have been there and in a small way participating in it.

William Kelly, RCAF

I've always felt good about it — I still feel good about it, I'm glad I can say that I was there. Made it more possible for the country to grow. You felt as though this is something out of the ordinary and the nice feeling it was to get out of the airplane when you landed back at base and you felt the satisfaction that this was something important.

Wilf Delaurie. (2003)

Wilf Delaurie, 1st Canadian Parachute Battalion

Right now I am very glad that I was there. Now I am also pleased that I'm still here. I feel very lucky that I did manage to go through that and I never really got a scratch at all.

Jim Parks, Royal Winnipeg Rifles

Jim Parks. (2003)

You knew what your job was going in, and to participate and to survive it was a great thing. But to see so many people who didn't make it, that's the traumatic thing to see. Afterwards you look at the names of the people and you say, "Oh, I remember him, I remember him," and you remember him as he was. You see pictures of people and you say, "Oh, that's so-and-so," and you get that sort of sad feeling, even now when you look through in our regimental magazine.

Hal Whitten. (2003)

Hal Whitten, Royal Canadian Navy

When you go over there and see the cemeteries — you gotta drop a few tears, I'll tell you that. At the time I just felt, "Well, it's my duty to go." Other young guys were going and so I thought, "Well, I'm of age and they want recruits so I'll go." I don't know whether it was for king and country or not, or whether it was for the adventure. I wouldn't have missed it for the world.

Frank Ryan, North Shore (NB) Regiment

Well, I didn't play a very big role, but I'm not afraid to say that I was there, but I don't brag about it either. There's so many people who were never outside of New Brunswick and they're getting 100 percent disability pensions and they know more about D-Day than anyone else.

Charles Fosseneuve, 13th Field Artillery

I feel good that I came in and today I feel very good. I've seen the country where I landed — it took me a long time to come in. [This interview occurred during Charlie's first visit to Normandy since the war, in June 2003.]

Charles Fosseneuve. (2003)

Richard Rohmer, RCAF

Well, I'm extremely fortunate in three ways. One is to have been a participant in D-Day, and to have seen it from the best seat in the house, and to have survived. It was a time that shaped my life. I have several careers, but the military aspect, it's a significant one for me. It was a pivotal lifetime event for me. I've written about it, I speak about it, and it was just an incredible experience. D-Day in the history of Canada must be one of the really significant turning points. A lot of attention is now being paid to D-Day sixty years after the event — probably more than has been in the past.

Richard Rohmer. (2003)

Ernie Jeans, 1st Canadian Parachute Battalion

I often thought afterwards that the people who came in on the beaches facing withering fire were much worse off than my particular experience. The day itself had this rather strange beginning for me and then the few early hours of the morning were kind of uneventful. I think it was an honour for me to have been a participant in this particular battle. There were

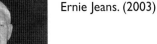

Ernie Jeans. (2003)

only five hundred or six hundred of us that had this opportunity to jump. I have an inner feeling of pride that I did this. I'm not so sure that the average person really realizes how much our generation, and, of course, the generation preceding us, did for Canada in those two dreadful wars. Out of the approximately six hundred people that jumped that day, when we returned to England in September there was less than three hundred of us left — a terrible sacrifice of young people.

Don Learment, North Nova Scotia Highland Regiment

I feel very, very fortunate to have come out of it with only a couple of minor scrapes and bruises and nothing to hospitalize me. No serious wounds at all. And I also felt very privileged to have been chosen by the colonel of the North Novas to lead the advance guard of the vanguard. I was only twenty-four, and though I didn't think of it at the time, I realize now that I was pretty fortunate to be put in command at that age of a group that large.

Jack Read, Royal Regina Rifles

Well, I think it is a memorable one and we all participated in some form or another. As you look back at it, the thought comes to mind about what took place and how fortunate it was that we were there and that we did manage to put up a pretty good fight.

Charles McNabb. (2003)

Charles McNabb, Queen's Own Rifles

Nobody should go through this again. What we did was fantastic, and I think the Canadian Army proved they were one of the best in the world. They're bad memories and I feel so bad that we lost such a lot of good men — chums we played ball with in England, chummed together, went to parties together. You try to remember them all, you try to remember their names, but you can't do it as you get older. Your memory is not as good as it was then. But believe me, I wouldn't want the next generation to go through this. Never again. Never.

John Dionne, 17th Hussars

Well, I feel very proud of myself, and I feel very, very proud of my two brothers. The three of us were all overseas. My eldest brother, he had joined the Royal Canadian Air

Force, he was in the Alouette Squadron. He was a flying officer, a pilot, and he got decorated by the King with the DFC. My other brother was in the RMR [Royal Montreal Regiment], he joined the RMRs I think the day that the war was declared. He was stationed in London at Army Headquarters. We all made it back — the three of us.

John Turnbull, RCAF

I wish there was some way in which I could express our feelings. Very, very proud. I am certainly proud that I had two brothers that were very much involved in the air force as well, in Bomber Command. We were involved in the war because we wanted to help people — they needed help, so our governments were there to do it and we were there to back them up.

John Turnbull. (2003)

Ken Hill, RCAF

I think there was a lot of patriotism in those years. When we would hear a band go by we'd get goosebumps, our hair would stand up on the back of our necks, and many kids like myself were afraid that the war would be over probably before we were old enough to get into it.

Ken Hill. (2003)

Francis Godon, Royal Winnipeg Rifles

We were young, most of us young fellas. It was our duty because Canada was our country and we wanted to save our people and try and help the other countries. I think we should be proud to be Canadians, and for my part being a Métis veteran, I wanted to prove that I could be just as good a soldier as everyone else. To do my duty, that was my job. It was important for my country and for the rest of the countries.

Francis Godon. (2003)

Arthur John Allin, 14th Field Regiment

We were quite young, all of us, and we were well trained. We were as prepared as troops could be. I don't know about everybody else, but I know damn well that I was a little bit scared, wondering what was going to happen. But nobody would show it at all because of the other guys, you don't want them to think you weren't as brave as the rest of them. The strength and the bond from the fighting and the risking of life and limb made a bond that still exists. It was one of the eventful dates in my life and I'm sure it was with anybody else that went in there.

Joe Oggy. (2003)

Joe Oggy, Queen's Own Rifles

Oh yes, I thought it was very important to do what we did. We've done our share after it's all over. I'm quite proud of the fact that we did a job to the best of our ability. We did very well — we did *very* well. The Queen's Own did a good job, I've very proud of them.

I'm quite glad I was part of it and I know that Canadians would do the same thing that I did and like the other boys if they had to.

Philip John Cockburn, 1st Hussars

It feels good, not everybody can do that. At that time it didn't feel any different really, but then later it became more important and it was the biggest operation yet, and then your mind starts to say, wait a minute, this was much bigger than I thought it was. Proud? We were, really, but when you stop to think that one tank made it against ten tanks that didn't — we felt we did the best job that we could do.

Jack Martin. (2003)

Jack Martin, Queen's Own Rifles

My brother was in the regiment with me, and we both survived. I'm very, very proud. There's an awful lot of blood in them beaches there. We got rid of Hitler — someone had to do it. As far as I knew and watched, the Canadians were the best damn soldiers that there were. Our guys landed without tank support — they were the only unit that didn't have any tank support. They landed tanks way far away and they had to come a way around 'til they got into Bernières, but by the time they arrived at Bernières the beach defences were gone and overrun by the boys. We lost the most men.

Bob Dale, RCAF

I did have a lot of friends killed in Normandy. We were just at that age and practically our whole graduating class went into the service out of high school. The same for those who got down to the first year of university — they practically all disappeared into the service. I think it means a lot to Canadians because so many people were involved.

Bob Dale. (2003)

August Herchenratter, Highland Light Infantry

We had to get those people who wanted to take over the world — the Germans with Hitler — and that's why I feel that it was an important engagement. I feel it was my duty, that's what we went in the army for. We stopped them and I'm thankful that I was among those who helped to stop them.

August Herchenratter. (2003)

Ed Reeve, Armoured Corp HQ

D-Day is something that our country ought to remember. These people that are lying here [Beny-sur-Mer cemetery] — these are the guys that did it. These are the people that have to be honoured. It is our duty to honour them, they gave it their everything.

Ed Reeve. (2003)

Mark Lockyer, 1st Canadian Parachute Battalion

We felt we were doing the right thing — of course we were. But what proved it when we were going through Germany, just outside of Hamburg, one of the concentration camps called Bergen Belsen — they had killed many Jews. And as our brigadier said, if you want to know what we are fighting for, that's a good place to see it. The reason I joined the army in 1942 was because my brother-in-law who married my oldest sister, he was taken prisoner at Dieppe. I felt it was my family duty to get involved and help liberate him.

Mark Lockyer. (2003 and 1944)

Beny-sur-Mer. (2003)

Douglas Lavoie, Fort Garry Horse

I've got to say that things have picked up since 1994, the fiftieth anniversary. We can't just blame our country for the fact that we've been so quiet about it. You can blame me, you can blame almost every veteran — that we never talked about it. I started talking about it a lot since 1994, the first time I went back. It seems that veteran after veteran has the same story: we never told our kids, we never talked about it. Why? I don't know. Maybe we got the impression that people don't want to hear about the war, but we were wrong. Our kids wanted to hear about it, people in Canada wanted to hear about it, and wanted to hear what we had to say. I was on *Cross Country Check Up* [CBC Radio] in 1994, and a lot of people heard me. One of my granddaughters who I never really got along that great with — when I got home she hugged me and she said, "Grandpa, I was so proud of you." Well, she was proud of me, but there was a tear in Grandpa's eye.

Left: The Canadian War Cemetery at Beny-sur-Mer, where many of the Canadian soldiers who gave their lives on D-Day are buried.

Right: Douglas Barrie. (2003)

Doug Barrie, Highland Light Infantry

It was the start of the end of the war. We had to land and we had to take and fight the land battles to complete the war. We did have a say in it, we had a part in it, and I'm just sorry that so many of our good fellas, so many of my friends and fellas that I lived with, trained with, fought with, and so on, did not come through. The ones I can think of — they were the best friends, the best soldiers that I ever knew and they didn't have the chance to come back to live a normal life, to have families, to have a job, to enjoy all the benefits we as Canadians have today. That's what makes me so sad, especially when I go over the lists and think of the many friends that are still there and never had a chance.

**Rolph Jackson,
Queen's Own Rifles**

I go to the cemetery at Beny-sur-Mer, in the far left corner. All my friends are there. I figure in that cemetery I know eighty people by first name. We find that the people in Normandy, particularly the villages that were liberated in the early stages of the war, they can't do enough for you.

Jan de Vries, 1st Canadian Parachute Battalion

Jan de Vries. (2003 and 1944)

I spent almost my whole life having survived all that and hardly give it a thought. It's only in the last few years, I guess because I'm older and retired, and all of a sudden I am beginning to think: I was damn lucky. And knowing from my own relatives in Holland — what they went through there, and what the French went through, and what the Belgians went through — what a magnificent thing it was that so many Canadians volunteered to go over there and stop this.

Ranville War Cemetery is the final resting place of the airborne troops who gave their lives on the east flank. Many members of the 1st Canadian Parachute Battalion are buried there. (2003)

People today have no idea where this guy Hitler was going. We were beginning to hear the stories when so many volunteered and put on the uniforms — never mind just the Jewish people whose stories were coming back, what was happening within those countries. That they were just grabbed off the street, put into factories to work for the Germans, grabbed to do the work in the fields for the Germans. They thought that they were

Top and Bottom Left and Right: Ranville. (2003)

the master race — that they were the only rightful people to rule the world. That was the philosophy that this Hitler had sold to the German people — and they were buying it. When he came to power and every kid and every schoolteacher was teaching them this philosophy, they bought it wholesale. And those kids at the beginning of the war were young teenagers now and became the best soldiers they had. That's where they got so many SS and excellent troops.

Did we save the world? Darn near it. Who knows how it would have turned out. I'm pleased and thankful that I survived and now I think more about all the guys who didn't — what would they have done with their lives if they'd have survived? We had so many guys that became doctors, engineers, teachers. And what about all the 144 that we lost? What could they have done for the country if they had survived?

Roy Shaw, Queen's Own Rifles

Roy Shaw. (2003)

I think it was an exceptional thing because since the war I have read the Anne Frank story where she mentioned that most of the general public thought that this was just going to be another repeat of Dieppe and they said the Germans are too strong — she said what was the general consensus was at that time. Certainly we had great odds against us, but I think we had God with us.

JUNO BEACH CENTRE

www.junobeach.org

On June 6, 2003, the official opening ceremonies of the Juno Beach Centre finally gave the Canadian veterans of the Second World War the memorial and museum they so richly deserved.

The opening ceremonies drew a crowd of thirty-five hundred people, including Canadian Prime Minister Jean Chrétien, French Prime Minister Jean-Pierre Raffarin, and a host of other dignitaries from Canada and France. Most importantly, there were one thousand Canadian veterans on hand. It was a heartwarming moment when these heroes were recognized by a

Left: Prime Minister Jean Chrétien speaks at the opening ceremonies of the Juno Beach Centre on June 6, 2003.

Right: The guests of honour at the opening ceremonies of the Juno Beach Centre.

The audience applauds the parade of the veterans during the opening ceremonies of the Juno Beach Centre.

Overall view of the Juno Beach Centre from Mike Red beach (taken prior to the opening, June 3, 2003).

Beautiful lines and stunning architecture brighten the oceanfront at Courseulles-sur-Mer.

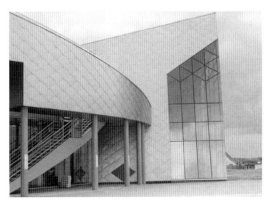

lengthy standing ovation during their parade. They were the reason the centre was built. Front and centre was D-Day veteran artilleryman Garth Wells, the man who conceived the idea of the Juno Beach Centre and who then, against all odds and countless naysayers, went on to bring this magnificent Canadian edifice into existence.

The Juno Beach Centre stands as a permanent shrine to all that Canadians did in the Second World War. Located at Courseulles-sur-Mer, just off of Mike Sector, where so many members of the Royal Winnipeg Rifles fell, the centre is an astonishing structure of outstanding design and original style.

The building is situated on a 1.5-hectare site, with permanent exhibits, temporary exhibits, an educational area, a gift shop, and offices. Outside are columns inscribed with the names of veterans, citizens, and companies who supported the building of the Juno Beach Centre. The fundraising for the centre, organized by Wells and his life partner, Lise Cooper, was spearheaded by the private sector and led by a committee of veterans, family members of veterans, and dedicated citizens. Major contributors included the governments of Canada, British Columbia, and Ontario; Wal-Mart was a main corporate participant. Such an initiative speaks volumes about the Canadian spirit.

Designed by Canadian Brian Chamberlain, the Juno Beach Centre has a unique shape that is essentially a pentagon with sloping segments that come together in the centre. The overall shape was chosen to reflect both the design of the Order of Canada and the outline of the maple leaf. The centre shimmers with its titanium surface and angled windows, creating a distinct presence on the shoreline. It is a dazzling structure that captures one's attention, while making a bold statement at one of the most important sites in Canadian history.

In the courtyard outside the centre stands the eight-foot bronze memorial sculpture "Remembrance and Renewal." Created by Colin Gibson, it depicts five figures in steel helmets, wound together in unity yet maintaining a sharp lookout from all sides. It dominates the courtyard and draws attention to the symbolism of the entire site. The centre boasts a large and airy entrance hall, complete with a reception area and a gift shop that offers military books, videos, and memorabilia as well as Canadian souvenirs, local keepsakes from Normandy, and Juno Beach Centre apparel.

Left: Juno Beach Centre: the main foyer.

Right: Juno Beach Centre: the gift shop, adjacent to the main foyer.

Visitors to the permanent exhibit are first greeted with a unique four-minute multimedia presentation chronicling the Canadian D-Day landing on Juno Beach. It is a powerful collage of still photographs and film footage, combined with audio clips to help establish the mood of the exhibits to come.

Left: Juno Beach Centre: "Canada In the 1930s" display section.

Right: Juno Beach Centre: the floor map with monitors in the "Canada In the 1930s" section.

The next room is a look at Canada in the 1930s, reflecting the experience of life in the various regions across the country. From vintage film footage to murals and displays, the room conveys what Canada was like in the years preceding the Second World War. Immigration, geography, agriculture, industry, and leisure — all are covered effectively and with a flair for the unusual. A map of Canada with monitors showing footage of each region covers the centre of the floor.

Juno Beach Centre: the radio room.

A hallway filled with vintage radios takes you back to an era when the family gathered around to hear news events break over the airwaves. Each radio has a photograph hung over it depicting the person whose speech is being heard. The important speeches of that era by Hitler, King George VI, Prime Minister Churchill, and Prime Minister William Lyon Mackenzie can be heard from each of the radios, giving voice to historical personages in the way that Canadians at the time would have heard them.

From there the next segment of the exhibit is entitled "Canada Goes to War." This room depicts Canada's war effort and shows how an entire nation mobilized in support of it, from agriculture and industry to the military. The various early battles that Canadians fought in are on display: the Battle of the Atlantic, the Battle of Britain, Dieppe, and the Battle of Hong Kong.

Juno Beach Centre: "Canada Goes To War" display section.

The tour continues to the "Roads to Victory" room, where displays cover the five major Canadian campaigns in Europe, with excellent vintage items available for viewing. From D-Day to V-Day, this room explains the role played by the various Canadian units involved, with superb visual presentations of the men themselves, relating their experiences.

To memorialize the men who made the ultimate sacrifice, the next room is entitled "Some Came Back, Others Did Not …" This area is a sombre reminder of the Canadian lives that were lost in the conflict. There are displays of personal effects as well as stories told through "look, listen, and learn" interactive booths.

The tour ends with a large room that celebrates the faces of Canada today. This room reflects Canada's diversity and achievements and acts as an inducement for Canadian tourism. The room has a huge window with a spectacular view of the landing beaches — a reminder of what it was that was fought for on D-Day

The Juno Beach Centre also has a consultation room with numerous computers so that visitors can access the materials available online at www.junobeach.org.

The Juno Beach Centre is a fitting tribute to the Canadians who made such huge personal sacrifices for their country and for the world. It acts as both a memorial and an educational centre about the Canadian role in the Second World War — one that will perpetuate the memory of our soldiers for generations to come.

Juno Beach Centre: "Roads to Victory" section, the 1st Canadian Parachute Battalion display.

Juno Beach Centre: "Some Came Back" display section.

Juno Beach Centre: "Faces Of Canada Today" section.

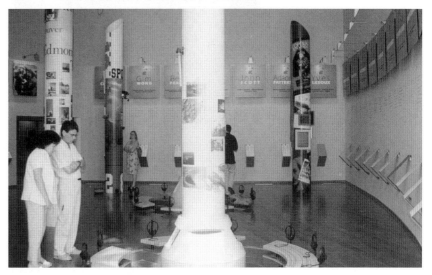

Left: The opening cere-
monies of the Juno Beach
Centre on the 59th anniversary of D-Day, June 6, 2003.

Right: The opening cere-
monies of the Juno Beach
Centre.

Left: Juno Beach Centre:
infantry uniform and weapon
display in the "Canada Goes
To War" section.

Top Right: Juno Beach
Centre: visitors on the first
day watching a video moni-
tor in the "Canada Goes To
War" section.

Bottom Right: Juno Beach
Centre: paratrooper's gear
on display in the "Roads To
Victory" section.

Left: Juno Beach Centre:
Canada at D-Day display
in the "Roads To Victory"
section.

Right: The Juno Beach
Centre, days prior to
its opening ceremonies.
(June 3, 2003)

GLOSSARY

Landing Craft

DUKW: Amphibious Vehicle
Size: 31' long, 8' wide, 2 1/2 tons
Cargo: 25 troops

LCA: Landing Craft, Assault
Size: 40' long
Cargo: 30 troops

LCI (L): Landing Craft, Infantry (Large)
Size: 158' 6" long, 23'8" wide
Cargo: 200 troops (388 maximum)
Troops would descend using ramps on either side of the bow.

An LCA being lowered from HMCS *Prince Henry* on D-Day.

LCI (L) 299 at Bernières-sur-Mer.

LCT (4) 1006 off Nan
White beach on D-Day.

LCT (Mk6): Landing Craft, Tank (Mark 6)
Size: 116' 5" long, 32' wide
Cargo: 4 tanks

Reinforcements going
ashore in LCAs and LCVPs
on D-Day

LCVP: Landing Craft, Vehicle, Personnel
Size: 35' long, 10' 10" wide
Cargo: 36 troops

LSI: Landing Ship, Infantry
Size: 500' long
Cargo: 6 LCAs, 2 LCMs, 550 troops
Their role was to get within a few kilometres of the landing beach
and to launch the LCAs and LCMs.

LST: Landing Ship, Tank
Size: 328' long, 50' wide
Cargo: 1 LCT, 18 tanks, 160 troops

Aircraft

Armstrong Whitworth
Albermarle on the runway.

Albermarle
Size: 77' wingspan, 59' 11" long, 15' 7" high
Maximum takeoff weight: 36,500 pounds
Maximum speed: 265 miles per hour
Range: 1,300 miles
Crew: 6

Armament: 4 machine guns, 4,500 pounds payload (or 10 paratroopers)

A bomber-transport, also used to tow gliders

Beaufighter

Size: 57' 10" wingspan, 41' 8" long, 15' 10" high

Maximum takeoff weight: 25,200 pounds

Maximum speed: 318 miles per hours

Range: 1,470 miles

Armament: Various configurations, including machine guns, cannons, bombs, torpedoes, or rockets

A fighter-bomber.

Bristol Beaufighter on the Tarmac.

C-47 Dakota

Size: 95' wingspan, 64' 5-1/2" long, 17' 1" high

Maximum takeoff weight: 31,000 pounds

Maximum speed: 230 miles per hour

Range: 1,600 miles

Armament: none

Cargo: 20 paratroopers, 13,000 pounds of supplies

Carried personnel and cargo, towed gliders, and dropped paratroopers.

D-47 Dakotas lined up on the runway.

Focke Wulf 190

Size: 34' 5" wingspan, 29' long, 13' high

Maximum takeoff weight: 10,805 pounds

Maximum speed: 406 miles per hours

Range: 915 miles

Armament: 2 machine guns and 4 cannons (variations allowed for bombs and rockets)

German fighter aircraft.

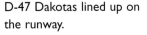

Focke Wulf Fw 190.

Handley Page Halifax in flight.

Halifax

Size: 98' 8" wingspan, 71' 7" long, 20' 9" high

Maximum takeoff weight: 68,000 pounds

Maximum speed: 282 miles per hours

Range: 1,985 miles

Armament: 5 machine guns, 14,500 lbs payload

Crew: 4

Long-range bomber.

Armstrong-Whitworth Albermarle aircraft towing a Horsa glider.

Horsa glider

Size: 88' wingspan, 68' long, 20' high

Maximum takeoff weight: 15,750 pounds

Load: 2 jeeps, or 1 jeep with anti-tank gun, ammunition, and crew, or 28 troops

Troop and material transport aircraft.

Hawker Hurricane.

Hurricane

Size: 40' wingspan, 32' 2" long, 13' 1" high

Maximum takeoff weight: 8,100 pounds

Maximum speed: 322 miles per hours

Range: 900 miles

Armament: 12 machine guns or 4 cannons

Fighter-bomber.

Junkers Ju88.

Junker Ju88

Size: 65'7" wingspan, 47'3" long, 15'11" high

Maximum takeoff weight: 30,865 pounds

Maximum speed: 280 miles

Range: 1696 miles

Armament: 7 machine guns, 7935 pounds payload

German heavy fighter-bomber.

Lancaster
Size: 102' wingspan, 69' 6" long, 20' 6" high
Maximum takeoff weight: 70,000 pounds
Maximum speed: 287 miles per hours
Range: 1,730 miles
Crew: 7
Armament: 3 machine guns, 12,000 pounds payload
Long-range bomber.

Avro Lancaster in flight.

Messerschmitt 109
Size: 32'4" wingspan, 28'4" long, 8'2" high
Maximum takeoff weight: 5,875 pounds
Maximum speed: 357 miles per hours
Range: 410 miles
Armament: 2 machine guns and 2 cannons
German fighter aircraft.

Messerschmitt Bf 109.

Mosquito
Size: 54' 2" wingspan, 44' 6" long, 12' 5-1/2" high
Maximum takeoff weight: 23,000 pounds
Maximum speed: 415 miles per hours
Range: 2,450 miles
Armament: none
Reconnaissance aircraft; its wooden frame made it hard to detect
on radar.

De Havilland Mosquito
in flight.

Mustang P-51A
Size: 37' wingspan, 32'3" long, 12'2" high
Maximum takeoff weight: 13,000 pounds
Maximum speed: 330 miles per hours
Range: 600 miles
Armament: 8 machine guns
Fighter aircraft.

Mustang aircraft in flight.

Supermarine Spitfire in flight.

Spitfire

Size: 36'10" wingspan, 29' 11" long, 11'5" high

Maximum takeoff weight: 8,500 pounds

Maximum speed: 448 miles per hour

Range: 470 miles

Armament: 2 cannons, 2 machine guns

The pre-eminent RCAF fighter aircraft of various marks.

Hawker Typhoon.

Typhoon

Size: 41' 7" wingspan, 31' 11" long, 15' 4" high

Maximum takeoff weight: 13,250 pounds

Maximum speed: 412 miles per hour

Range: 980 miles

Armament: 4 cannons (earlier versions had 12 machine guns)

A potent anti-tank fighter-bomber and rocket carrier.

Weapons

Bangalore

A metal pipe filled with explosives, used to clear barbed wire or minefields, usually in sections to allow for it to be detonated at a distance

BAR

Browning automatic rifle

Bren gun display. (Merville battery museum, 2003)

Bren gun

Size: 115 centimetres long, 10 kilograms

.303 calibre, 30 round magazine, 500 rounds per minute

DD Tank
Duplex Drive Tank
Custom fitted with inflatable gear, canvas siding, and propellers to allow the tanks to float and approach shore on their own.

DD tank, deflated and with canvas down, in action.

Piat gun
Projector, Infantry, Anti-tank (short range anti-tank gun)
Size: 99 centimetres long, 14.5 kilograms
Range: 90 metres

Piat gun being used in a training drill.

Sten gun
Size: 30" long, 7 pounds
9 mm automatic, 32 round magazine, 550 rounds per minute

Sten gun resting on the hood of the jeep.

Other Terms

CP   command post

CO   commanding officer

DZ   Drop Zone

E-Boat   German torpedo boat

FOO   Forward Observation Officer

Mulberry   Floating prefabricated port that was shipped across the English Channel and used at the beaches in Normandy to supply/reinforce the invasion forces. Without Mullberry ports at Acromanches the Battle of Normandy could not have been won.

OP   observation post

RZ   Rendezvous Zone

Sapper   Military engineer who lays or detects and disarms mines

BIBLIOGRAPHY/ RESOURCES

Books

Ambrose, Stephen. *D-Day June 6, 1944: The Climatic Battle of World War II* (Touchstone, 1994).

Bernage, Georges. *The D-Day Landing Beaches: The Guide* (Heimdal, 2001).

Ford, Ken. *D-Day 1944, Volume 4: Gold & Juno Beaches* (Oxford: Osprey, 2002).

Fowler, Will. *D-Day: The First 24 Hours* (Lewis, 2003).

Jackson, Robert. *Aircraft Of World War II* (Silverdale, 2003).

Rohmer, Major General Richard. *Patton's Gap: Mustangs Over Normandy* (Toronto: Stoddart, 1981).

Resource Centres

Archives Normandie

Britannica On-Line

CBC News On-Line

Department of National Defence Canada

Imperial War Museum (UK)

Juno Beach Centre on-line resources (www.junobeach.org)

National Archives Canada

Normandie Memoire

University of San Diego (http://history.acusd.edu/gen/)

Veterans Affairs Canada

www.worldwar-2.net

ACKNOWLEDGEMENTS

AlarmForce, Joel Matlin, President (travel sponsor)

Captain Rita Arendz, Queen's Own Rifles of Canada

Department of National Defence Canada

Jan de Vries, 1st Canadian Parachute Battalion Association

Janice Summerby, Veterans Affairs Canada

Major General Richard Rohmer, Chair, the 60th Anniversary of D-Day Advisory Committee to the Minister of Veterans' Affairs

National Archives of Canada

Ray Coulson, North Nova Scotia Highlanders Museum

Roy Clarke, Aircrew Association

PHOTO INDEX

National Archives of Canada

Department of National Defence, Canada

Imperial War Museum, U.K.

INDEX OF THE MEN

ABOUT THE AUTHOR

Lance Goddard began his career in Toronto, working as a cameraman, editor, writer, director, and producer of shows, promotional ads, contests, and field-produced news. He was the winner of the Best Video of the Year award in 1985, a CAB award in 1986, and a CAB Gold Ribbon Award in 1989 for his work on *In Gilbert's Path*, a documentary on the devastation caused by Hurricane Gilbert. He was the 2000 recipient of the Barbara Frum National Media Award for his charitable work with Global Television on behalf of the Leukemia Research Fund of Canada.

In 2002 Lance produced the documentary *Victory from Above*, about the 1st Canadian Parachute Battalion. Aired originally on Remembrance Day of that year, forty thousand copies of the video and DVD were sold, making it one of the nation's most popular documentaries on WWII.

Dedicated to his children, *D-Day: Juno Beach, Canada's 24 Hours of Destiny* is as much a personal project as a professional one for Lance: his grandfather served in the British Army and fought in the Battle of Britain and in North Africa and Italy; his great-grandfather served in WWI and died from mustard gas; and his great-uncle was an engineer who designed parts of bomber aircraft in WWII.

Help preserve Canada's military and civilian contribution to WWII

Juno Beach Centre
Veteran and Donor Brick Program

To commemorate the sacrifice of Canadian WWII veterans, and to recognize the support of project donors, the Juno Beach Centre is offering the opportunity to purchase an engraved brick to be placed on the walls of a kiosk on the project's property on the beach of Courseulles-sur-Mer.

The veterans' bricks will include the person's rank, name, decorations, unit, and dates of service, as well as a comment regarding the veteran's service, such as "Italian Campaign," "Battle of the Atlantic," or "D-Day Veteran." These bricks will be mounted on the walls of one of several kiosks built near the entrance to the Centre.

The donors' bricks, mounted on the same kiosks but on separate panels from the veteran's bricks, will include the donor's name, optional organization information, and city and province of residence.

To purchase a Veteran or Donor Brick, please contact:

Juno Beach Centre
24-2407 Woodward Avenue
Burlington, ON
L7R 4J2
donations@junobeach.org
1-877-828-JUNO (1-877-828-5866)

You can also purchase a brick online at www.junobeach.org.